Laura Aguilar Tina Barney **Lisa Bartolozzi**
William Beckman **Brett Bigbee** Paul Cadmus
Sherry Camhy David Carbone **Harriet Casdin-Silver** Joe Cavallaro **Eteri Chkadua** Chuck Close
John Coplans **Renée Cox** Meg Cranston **James Croak** John Currin **Steven DiGiovanni** Jeanne Dunning **Karen Finley** Lucian Freud **Philip Grausman** Chris Habib **Anne Harris** Jacqueline Hayden **Kinke Kooi** Peter Krashes **Daniel Ladd**
Jacob Lawrence Harriet Leibowitz **Michael Leonard** Melanie Manchot **Denise Marika** John O'Reilly **Hanneline Røgeberg** Karin Sander
Jenny Saville Andres Serrano **Robert Stivers**
Annelies Štrba **Jock Sturges** Robert Taplin
Spencer Tunick **Manabu Yamanaka** Lisa Yuskavage

THE **NUDE** IN CONTEMPORARY ART

JUNE 6 – SEPTEMBER 12, 1999

THE **ALDRICH MUSEUM**

OF CONTEMPORARY ART

ISBN # 1-888332-10-7

© 1999 The Aldrich Museum of Contemporary Art
258 Main Street, Ridgefield, Connecticut 06877

Designed by Lisa Feldman Design, Inc.
Printed by Herlin Press, Inc.

Exhibition and education funding provided, in part,
by the Connecticut Commission on the Arts.

Education funding provided by: The Alexander Julian
Foundation for Aesthetic Understanding and Appreciation,
The O'Grady Family Foundation, The Perrin Family
Foundation, and The RJR Nabisco Foundation.

A portion of The Aldrich Museum's general operating
funds has been provided through a grant from the Institute
of Museum and Library Services, a Federal agency serving
the public by strengthening museums and libraries.

cover: John O'Reilly, *As An Apollo*, 1981

CONTENTS

ACKNOWLEDGMENTS

This exhibition has been curated in an attempt to focus on the deceptively simple idea in its title. I have been fortunate to collaborate on the curatorial process with Jessica Hough and Richard Klein, the Museum's assistant curator and assistant director respectively, to whom I am very grateful. They have contributed enormously in achieving whatever level of success the exhibition enjoys; however, any shortcomings or omissions in the selection of artists or works of art are entirely my own.

I am privileged to work closely with members of The Aldrich's Board of Trustees on the Museum's exhibition committee; they responded enthusiastically and quickly to the initial proposal to mount this exhibition.

Our thanks go to Karen Finley, whose work inspired this exhibition; The Aldrich is honored to work with an artist of her passion and achievement. Karen has added a wonderfully personal note to the catalogue with her brief reminiscence of the life drawing classes she attended in her youth. On behalf of The Aldrich, I would like to thank the Ridgefield

Guild of Artists, the Silvermine Guild Arts Center, and the Wooster Community Art Center for their assistance in organizing the drawing classes held as part of Karen Finley's *Go Figure*. Rafe Churchill and Aran Winterbottom have been invaluable in organizing the life drawing classes. Thanks to Julie Lazar and Brent Zerger at The Museum of Contemporary Art, Los Angeles for sharing their insight on *Go Figure* as it was held in Los Angeles.

Our thanks go especially to David McCarthy, who has ably put this exhibition into historical context in his insightful essay. We are pleased to work again with Lisa Feldman, whose smart and fresh design sense shapes this book.

We are grateful to all the galleries who helped us with this exhibition, and to all those who suggested artists to us. For their generous loans to this exhibition our deep gratitude goes to Joe Barron; Yvonne Force Inc.; T. Haddad and M. Dembowski; Wendy Evans Joseph; Martin Margulies; Hank Muchnic; The Museum of Modern Art, Arnhem; Nina Neilson; Rose Art Museum, Brandeis University; Robert Roth; Robert D. Summer and Susan Kasen Summer; and Mr. P. G. Van Deursen. Special thanks to Harrison Jenkins Design and Joseph Merritt & Co., Hartford for their help with Melanie Manchot's billboard project.

I would like to most especially thank all the participating artists whose work carries forward one of the great traditions of art, the nude. —Harry Phibrick

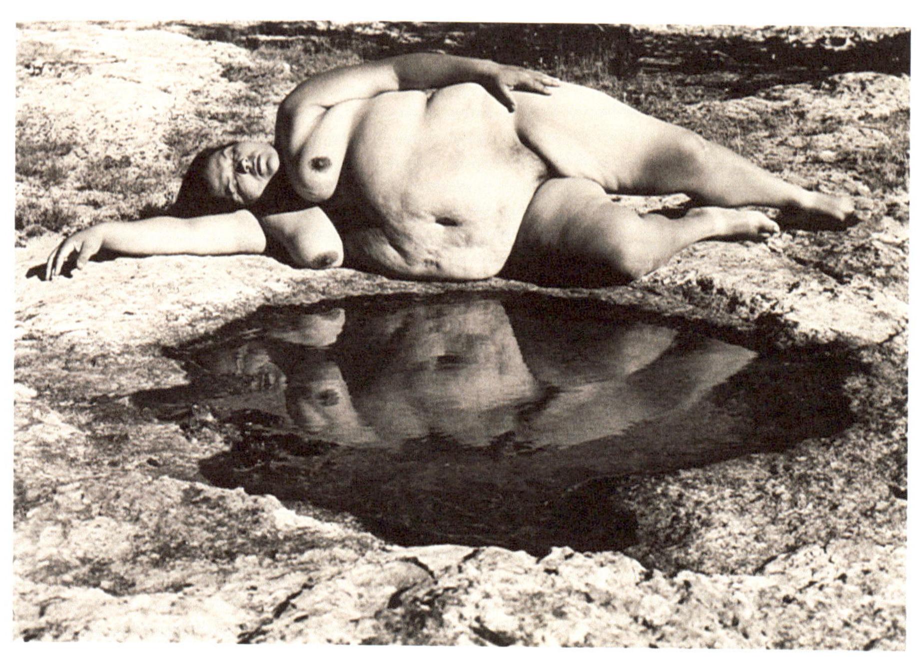

Laura Aguilar

Nature Self-Portrait No. 4, 1996

THE NUDE IN OUR TIME

A BRIEF RUMINATION ON THE NUDE IN CONTEMPORARY ART
— HARRY PHILBRICK

WE LIVE IN STRANGE TIMES WHEN IT COMES to nudity. For example, how does a contemporary artist, a feminist, end up feeling more comfortable having a conversation with an executive of *Playboy* magazine than with an art world insider? This brief essay will explore this question, and others relating to *The Nude in Contemporary Art*. My starting point will be the genesis of the exhibition, and the aforementioned artist, Karen Finley.

This exhibition was born out of a series of conversations with Karen, who had been scheduled to create a new work for *HERE*, an exhibition of site-specific installations at The Aldrich in September of 1998. Several months before the opening Karen called me to say that she wouldn't be able to participate. Karen had worked with The Aldrich on a number of occasions in the past, and we agreed that when the time was right, we would work together again. At that time her long-running court case, *Finley et al v. National Endowment for the Arts,* which challenged the NEA's application of so-called "decency tests" to artist's grants, was nearing its conclusion in the United States Supreme Court.

In late June 1998 the Supreme Court ruled in favor of the government, upholding the constitutionality of Congress requiring the NEA to take into account the "general standards of decency and respect for the diverse beliefs and values of the American public." This appeared to be a classic case of an artist seeking the right to freely express herself, no matter how controversial that expression might be, versus a government seeking to muzzle her. In fact the case, and the verdict itself, was a little less clear cut. According to Jeffrey Cunard, Counsel to the College Art Association, one of the plaintiffs in the case, the verdict was "not nearly so damaging to the interests of artists as had been feared."[1] The majority opinion, written by Justice Sandra Day O'Connor, concluded that the government was not prohibiting the funding of certain speech, that the "decency and respect" clause was only "advisory language."[2]

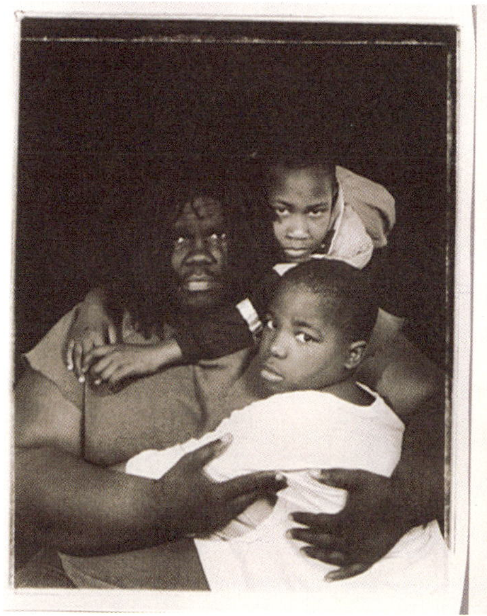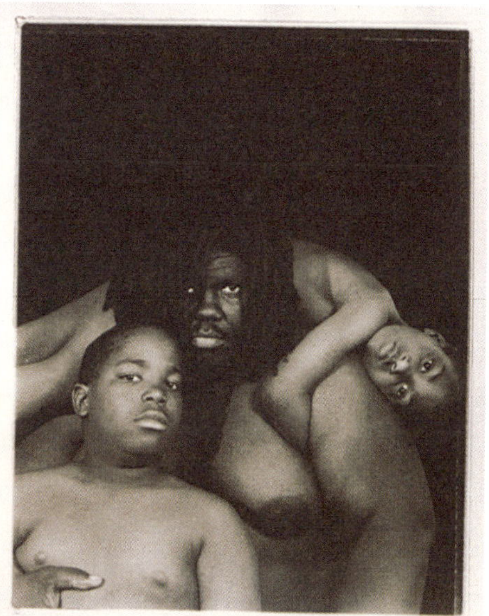

Laura Aguilar

Clothed / Unclothed Series No. 34, 1994

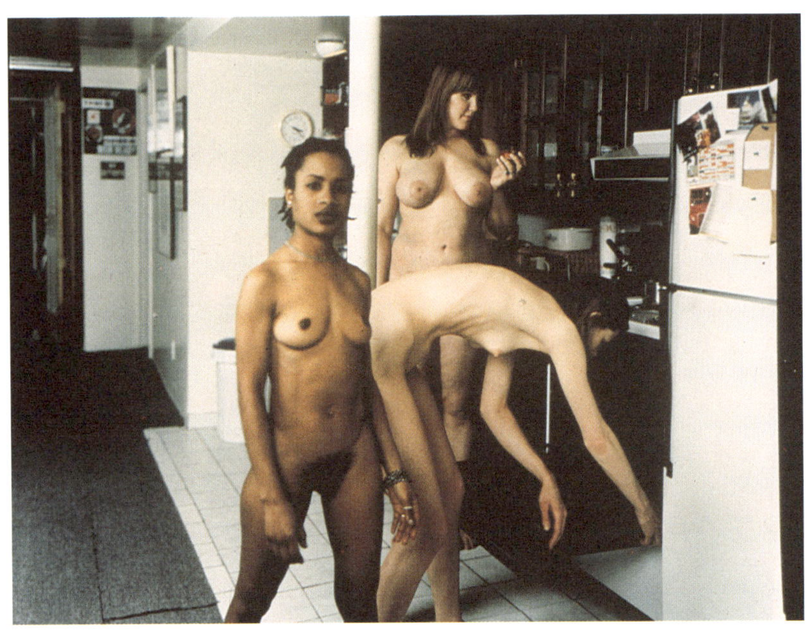

Tina Barney

Nude #1045, 1996

The true impact of the decision will only be revealed over time. When the verdict was announced, however, the headlines were clear: Karen Finley had "lost," and the NEA had "won." For Karen, this was an enormous blow, the losing end to a struggle which had lasted for many years.[3] Shortly thereafter, on the Fourth of July, *The New York Times* ran an article by Mel Gussow under the headline, "The Whitney Cancels a Karen Finley Exhibition." The article stated:

The Whitney Museum of American Art has cancelled "The Great American Nude," an exhibition featuring the visual and performance art of Karen Finley that had been scheduled to open in December. ... [Willard Holmes, then the Whitney's acting director] said the decision had nothing to do with the content of Ms. Finley's contribution or any other part of the exhibition. Nor, he said, was the cancellation related to a United States Supreme Court ruling last week against Ms. Finley and three other performance artists."[4]

I knew from earlier conversations with Karen that her contribution to the Whitney's exhibition was to be *Go Figure*[5]. In fact, it was my understanding that the Whitney's exhibition had grown from a simple display of Karen's *Go Figure* into a larger exhibition. A few days after *The*

Times article ran I called Karen and asked if she would consider mounting *Go Figure* at The Aldrich as part of an exhibition by a range of contemporary artists dealing with the nude. Karen agreed, and shortly thereafter the Museum's exhibition committee approved the idea, and the curatorial process began.

Our press release announcing this exhibition led to a further article by Mel Gussow in *The Times* on August 13, and numerous articles in the local press about the exhibition. While this press attention was gratifying, it began to illuminate for me the strange ways in which our culture currently deals with the most basic and essential aspect of our physical existence, our bodies.

It is a simple truism, oft repeated, that we are bombarded with suggestive images of models and media celebrities in various degrees of undress. We seem, as a culture, to be accepting of these images, and they seem to aid in the selling of many different products, and to provide much entertainment in films, magazines, and on television and the internet. However, when the human body is the subject of a work of art, we become much less sure of our ground, and fearful that it perhaps may be something inappropriate for our children to see. *The Ridgefield Press* captured the flavor of this uncertainty and its underlying fear

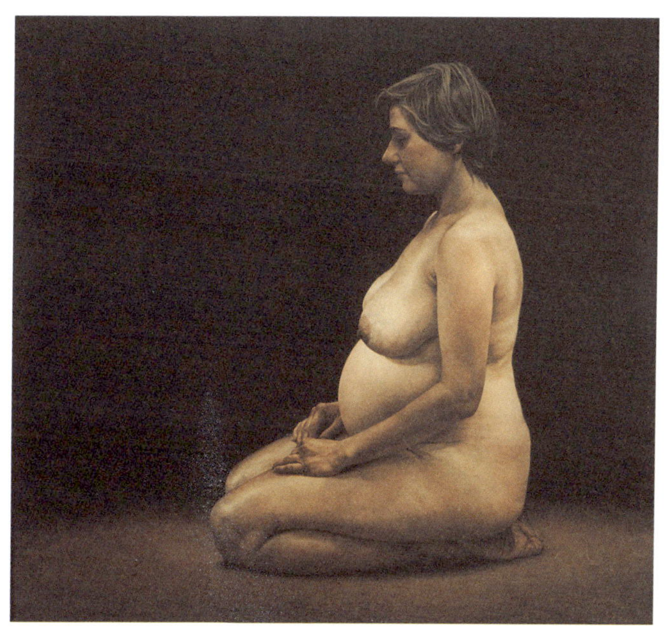

Lisa Bartolozzi

Wisdom, 1998

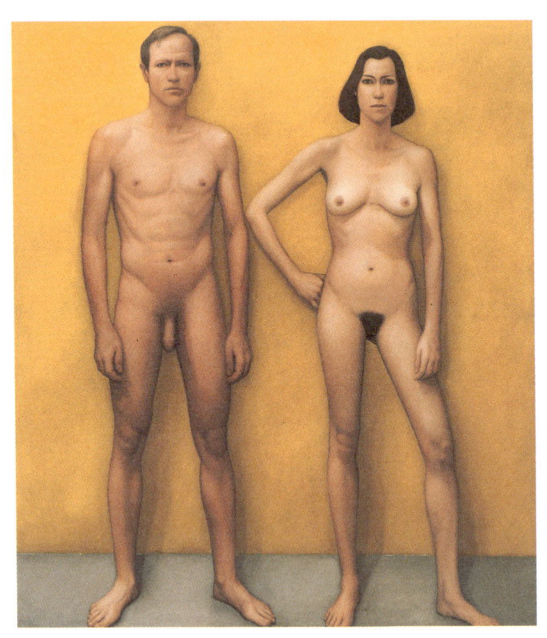

William Beckman

Yellow Painting (Man and Woman), 1991–96

beautifully in its August 27 headline, "Expelled nudes heading here." This headline brought to mind an image of a long, slow line of expelled nudes marching to Ridgefield, their fall from grace so complete as to render them some sort of undead, an unstoppable army descending on a defenseless town. Now, none of the magazines or videos available in town had provoked such headlines, so how could an exhibition of art, as yet uncurated, provoke such anxiety?

      In mulling over this question it is first gratifying to note that despite the cascading ascendance of various new media, and the dazzling array of images available in print, in cyberspace, over the airwaves, and in cinemas, old fashioned art still packs a potent punch. People are afraid that a still picture, hanging on the wall of a museum, might be a threat. As a museum administrator, I am delighted to think that the somewhat old-fashioned practice of gathering pictures and objects for contemplation still remains viable and powerful. Apparently viewers still expect more from art than from popular culture, so a work of art is given the benefit of the doubt; viewers expect that it may very well be important until proven otherwise.[6] This would explain why a *museum* exhibition of nudes might provoke attention where a magazine photo spread might not. But what of the *nude* itself? Whatever reason the Whitney had for canceling its exhibition, the decision drew reaction because it was an exhibition of nudes: it is hard to imagine another staple of art, such as landscape, provoking the same reaction. Why are we so uncomfortable in our own skin, or at least in depictions of our own skin?

A number of answers—ranging from a secret sense of shame about the exploitative uses to which the human body is put to an inability to believe that the nude and the sexually exploitative might not be inseparable—suggest that the flood of popular culture has obscured a great tradition in Western art. The nude has embodied many things in the history of Western art, from the Greek notion of the body's symmetry and balance representing an ideal upon which architectural order and proportion were based to the Surrealist use of the body—primarily female—as the site of desire, fear, and mystery. Whatever it might have symbolized at any given time, the nude has now fallen into a strange limbo, not banned outright, but not easily accepted as a legitimate icon for artistic use.

Karen Finley's *Go Figure* provides a means to examine this issue from a number of perspectives. *Go Figure* consists of a gallery in the Museum which has been converted into a life drawing classroom. Every day the exhibition is open there will be drawing classes, with a model and an instructor, open to any Museum visitor. Participants are invited

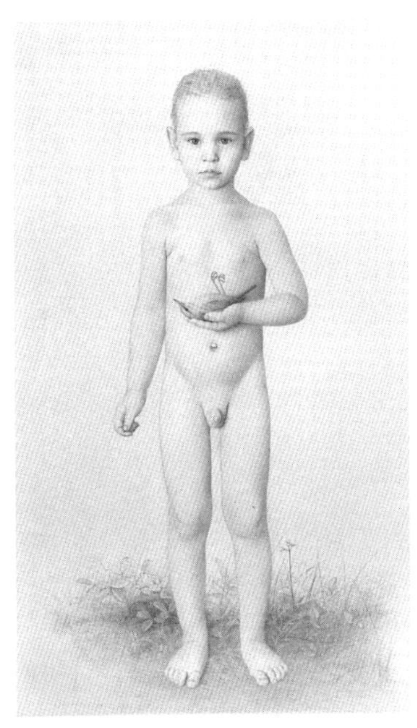

Brett Bigbee

Bird I, 1998

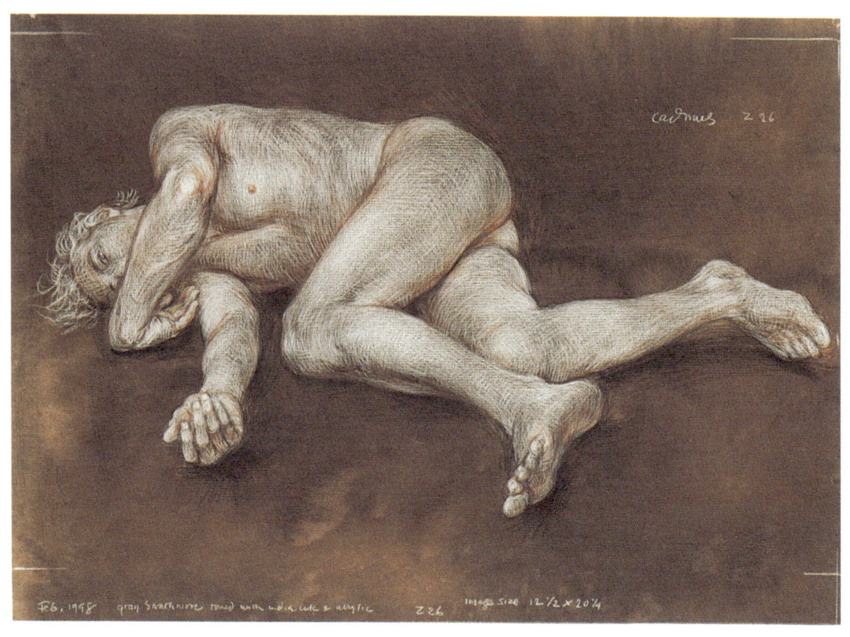

Paul Cadmus

Male Nude Z26, 1998

to pin their finished works on the walls of the gallery for public viewing. As with much of Karen's work, the very title *Go Figure* is a humorous concoction hiding a serious and open-ended assault on some of the accepted sensibilities of our age. There is the pun on figure drawing, and on figuring it out. The same thing that every traditional art class in America teaches, life drawing, is controversial if it is done in a contemporary art museum. *Go Figure.*

Karen's act of bringing the model and teacher into the Museum is a brilliant stroke, which at once undoes the traditional relationship between viewer, artists, artwork, and institution. It is an invitation, in some ways, for all the armchair quarterbacks to try it themselves, and to discover just exactly how hard it is to do it yourself. It is a wonderful demonstration of Joseph Beuys's idea that, for the visual artist, drawing *is* thinking. You try it, you think it through. *Go Figure.*

The preponderance of images of nudes we see are primarily pictures *by* men and *of* women, and while the mix is slowly changing to include more men as subjects, and more women as creators, the issue of whose gaze predominates is key in deciphering art and art history. In the drawing classes at the Museum you will never know whether to expect a male or female model, and those drawing will be both male and female. The decision to leave a drawing pinned to the wall of the gallery/classroom is voluntary. Whose vision will be on view? *Go Figure.*

Karen Finley has the uncanny ability to shock both the mainstream—she is often referred to, in the best tabloid headline style, as "the chocolate-smeared woman," after perhaps her most notorious performance—and the art world. Her recent decision to pose for *Playboy* magazine is a case in point. Karen felt that her work had been eroticised by the media, and decided to "go with that rather than fight it"; to try to turn the fear that erotic content would make her look unprofessional from a disadvantage into an advantage. The feminist art movement of the last thirty-five years or so has investigated issues revolving around identity and power, including the often subtle manifestations of male power, the male gaze, and the use of the female form in art and media. From Karen's perspective, the first "layer" of feminist art reclaimed female sexuality from men, but the second layer denied female sexuality, and put forward an image of women as victims. Her work, she feels, is now being created in a culture which deems women as "bad because they bring up sexual feelings"—thus perpetuating a notion of women as either a casualty or causality of evil.[7] For Karen to agree to pose for *Playboy*, and to be interviewed for the same issue, is a demonstration of her ability

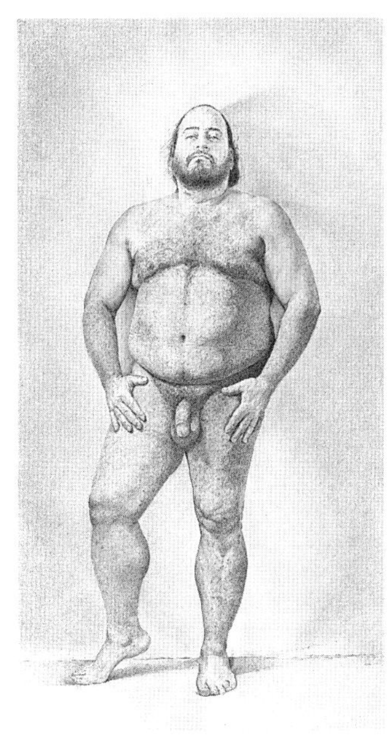

Sherry Camhy

Richard, The Golem, 1999

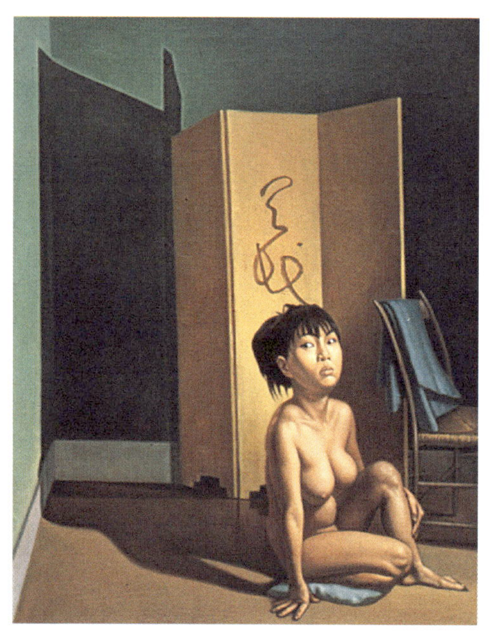

David Carbone

Visitation, 1995–96

to ask tough questions through her actions. She brings into question the hierarchy of depiction, and asks who is in control of her image? Is she artist or model? *Go Figure.*

Karen was surprised to find herself having conversations with executives at *Playboy* she wished she were having with people in the art world. The nude is a difficult subject for contemporary writers and critics to deal with simply. The baggage of the many discourses on sexuality and gender has obscured a simpler subject, the nude. While we may not be comfortable with the ideal associated with Kenneth Clark's nude, neither do we always hunger for the naked (see David McCarthy's accompanying essay). There is a middle ground, or perhaps an embrace of the real, a celebration of frankness, in much of the work in this exhibition. Few major museum exhibitions have focused on representations of the nude recently, as opposed to presentations of the body as a political or cultural staging ground. A paradox I have experienced as this show took shape is that while many people in the New York art world told me this is a bold and timely exhibition, many members of local artists' groups, such as the Ridgefield Guild of Artists, have implied that at last The Aldrich is exhibiting art that connects with their concerns, which they feel have been ignored in contemporary art for a long time.

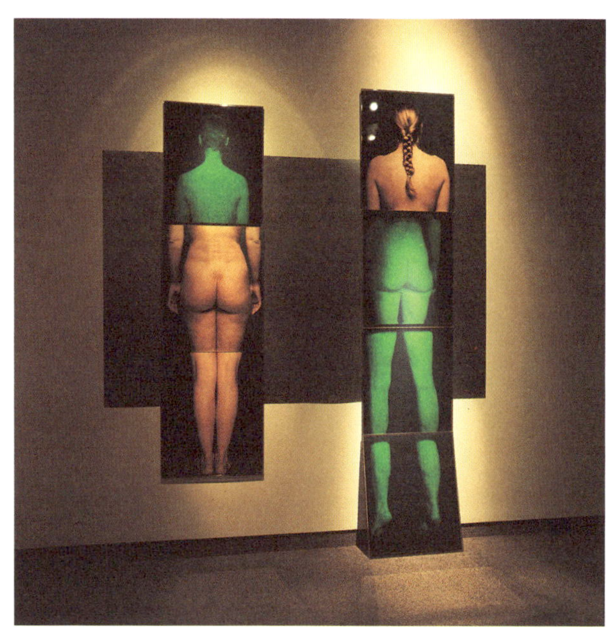

Harriet Casdin-Silver

To Soutine and Matisse, 1996

Look at Sherry Camhy's life-size drawing *Richard, The Golem* on page 23. There is nothing particularly erotic or politically charged about the piece; it is the straightforward nature of her depictions which give her work its strength. This frankness marks much of the work in this exhibition, and is, perhaps, at the core of why we respond so strongly to the nude: the nude is, at its best, still a clear mirror on ourselves as humans. Camhy, who teaches figure drawing at The Art Student's League in New York, commented to me that when her studio is open to the public as part of the West Chelsea Art Walk some visitors are audibly shocked at her straightforward, detailed drawings of male genitalia.[8] The penis is still a taboo in our culture; mainstream movies coyly omit male genitalia as a rule. But look again at Camhy's drawing: the model's confident, almost jaunty, pose indicates *he* is feeling no discomfort about his nudity, and nor, perhaps, should we. The face, which is almost always nude, is where our emotions are most consciously expressed; *Richard* is equally expressive through both face and body, which is the key to the success of the drawing.

This challenge of linking the (usually exposed) face to the (often covered) body underlies David McCarthy's point, in his accompanying essay, that "The fact so many nudes are banal, and have been for several centuries, underlies how difficult the subject remains." Our bodies famously reveal our animal selves, and we tend to think of this aspect of our nature in sexual terms. Yet our animal self is also manifested in the absolute ordinariness of our bodies, of their functional nature, and of the inevitable toll of time on our physical selves.

This stamp of our mortality, the inevitable toll of time on our posture, joints, skin, and hair, is graphically displayed in the disturbing images of Manabu Yamanaka. This, of course, is why the nude in art simply won't go away: the body is the seat of the soul, and as such can be the vehicle for much of what we hope art can express. It is no coincidence that the greatest iconic image of Christian art, the crucified Christ, depicts the body as the vessel for the spirit.

Notes

1. Jeffrey Cunard, "Legal Update," *CAA NEWS* Volume 23, Number 5 (September 1998), 11.

2. Ibid.

3. Karen Finley, in a conversation with the author, April 1999.

4. *The New York Times*, Arts & Ideas, Saturday, July 4, 1998.

5. A version of *Go Figure* was included in *Uncommon Sense*, an exhibition organized by Tom Finkelpearl and Julie Lazar at The Museum of Contemporary Art, Los Angeles in 1997.

6. This is a point which museums ignore at their own peril; to stray from the core mission of exhibiting and aiding in the interpretation of art is to invite irrelevancy. Attempts by museums to compete with other forms of entertainment will lead museums to compete in a game which they don't have the resources to win, and to ignore the one thing which gives them enduring importance: the actual objects on display. In an increasingly "virtual" world, this is truer than ever.

7. Finley, in a conversation with the author, April 1999.

8. Sherry Camhy, in a conversation with the author, April 1999.

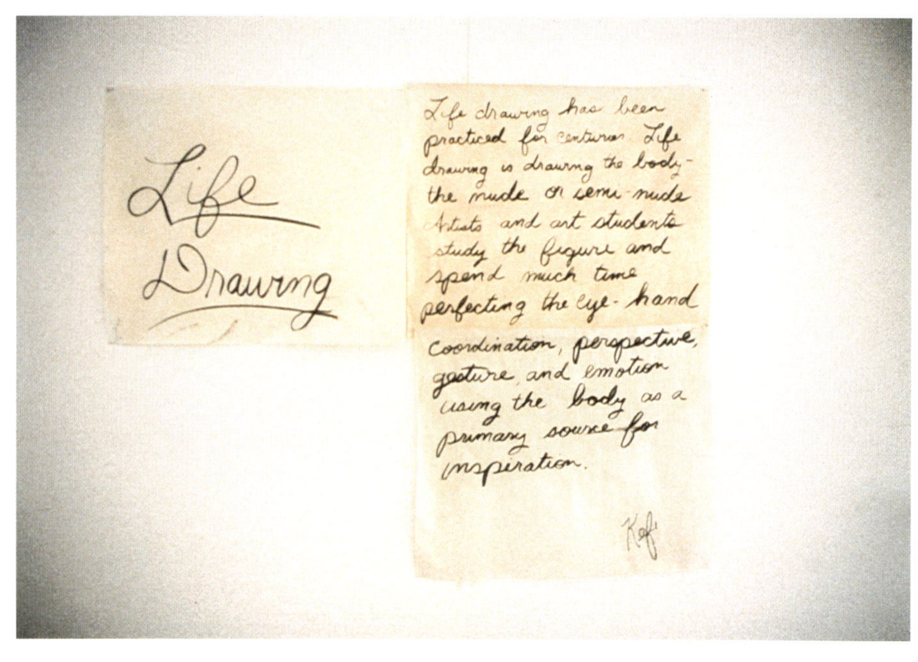

Karen Finley

Go Figure, Installation at MoCA at the Geffen Contemporary (detail), 1997

DRAWING FROM LIFE
— KAREN FINLEY

I WAS TWELVE YEARS OLD WHEN I STARTED Life Drawing Class with Emmanuel Jacobson at the Young Artists Studio at The Art Institute of Chicago.

The class began at 9:00 am and I had to be on the platform at South Boulevard to meet the elevated train to the Loop. Sometimes the weather was treacherous, with sleet, or heavy winds accompanied by snow. In order to avoid the weather, I would get off the subway at Adams, which had entrances to department stores, and make my way through the basement of Marshall Field's or admire the Louis Sullivan architecture of Carson Pirie Scott. The first time I went with my mother and the second time my mother and youngest brother, aged two, followed me without my knowing.

Now being a student at the Young Artists Studio at The Art Institute of Chicago certainly had its privileges—one of them being free membership to the museum and the ability to walk though the museum to enter the school. I would walk up the elegant entrance stairs with stone monumental lions, enter the museum, walk past the Asian collections with architecture on my right, a changing exhibit—whether Egon Schiele or paperweights—and past the Thorne Rooms (exact miniature replicas of famous and architectural rooms).

Mr. Jacobson was over fifty when I started drawing in his class. Once in his classroom it was all business. A table was set with an array of art supplies to choose—charcoal, oil pastel. I would always choose an ebony pencil, still my favorite drawing tool to this day.

We'd start with newsprint and thirty-second poses, and gradually do longer poses—one minute, three minutes, ten minutes, until finally our last pose of one hour. We would usually use a better piece of paper and more luscious art supplies for the one-hour pose. The model would usually pose herself/himself, but the decorative setting was fitting to

Mr. Jacobson's mood—floral geometric fabrics with bright garlands of fruit. The bodies would come in all sizes and shapes and ages and we, as children, deeply tried to capture their essence on our paper.

Mr. Jacobson would wear his grey smock with tie peeking out and instruct our eye-hand coordination on a deep spiritual level that provided me with a profound artistic awakening for my young life.

Being an artist in Mr. Jacobson's class was to take a vow; it was a responsibility, a not-to-be-taken-lightly commitment. This understanding of the creative act I carried with me through *Finley vs. NEA* to the Supreme Court. And it was the ethics involved in my early years of life drawing and the participation with the nude that brought about my life path with the arts.

Mr. Jacobson took me seriously as an artist and treated me with dignity and respect. His appreciation of the artist as professional I remembered during the culture wars and it gave me strength. Mr. Jacobson wrote to me after seeing me perform at the Jane Addams Hull House in Chicago. The famous chocolate performance. His letter, which I still have, meant so much to me.

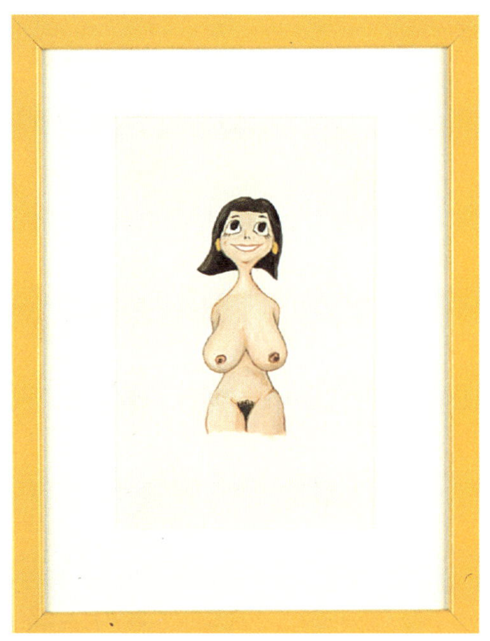

Joe Cavallaro

Small Nude Woman, 1994

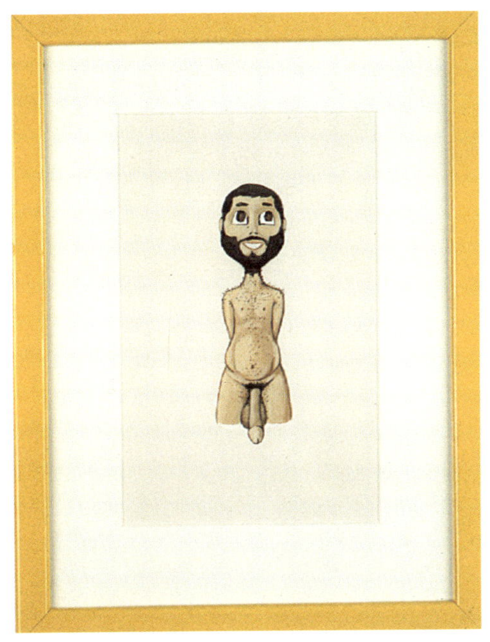

Joe Cavallaro

Small Nude Man, 1994

Eye-hand coordination, whether in drawing or hitting a baseball, takes a focus and tension that allows relaxation from the rest of the world's problems. This makes drawing Zen-like; the practice of life drawing, meditative—self reflective, spiritual without words—the body evokes a dance on paper.

Pain was brought out of me in the *Finley vs. NEA* case—but a major pain was that both other artists and myself were looked at as deviants, as out-of-control crazies trying to take advantage of the government and taxpayers' money.

Using the body as a source of inspiration has been done since the caves of Lascaux, the drawings of Lautrec—the body interpreted at a point in time to evoke a feeling of the human condition.

Looking back I never remembered once any crude or sexual remark, or any inhibition in reference to the nude model or in drawing the model. The class was purely a complement to the connecting museum that housed nudes of all seven continents in all media. Just as gymnasts and musicians start as children to learn their craft, we as young artists learned ours.

—Karen Finley, Los Angeles, April 1999

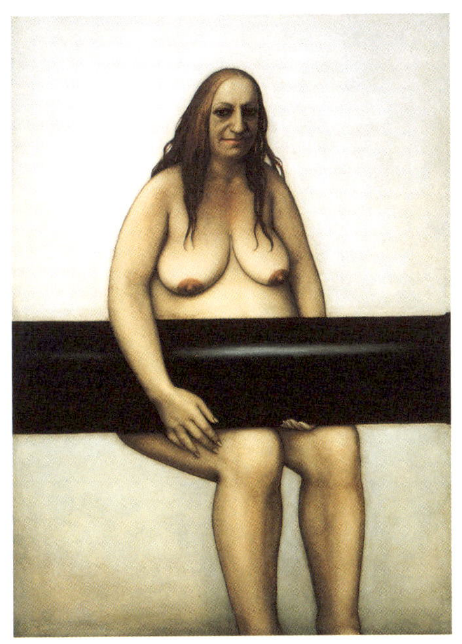

Eteri Chkadua

Janna, 1992

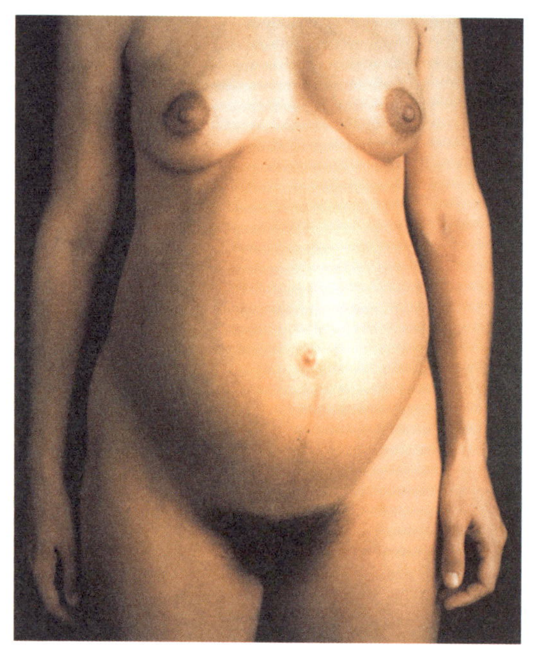

Chuck Close

© Torso I & II, 1999

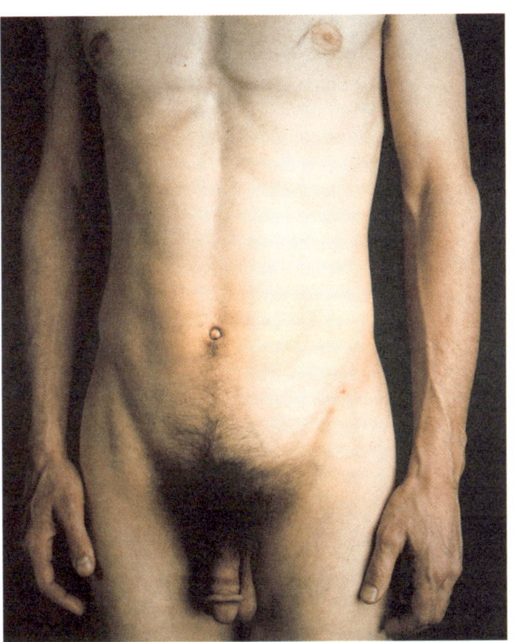

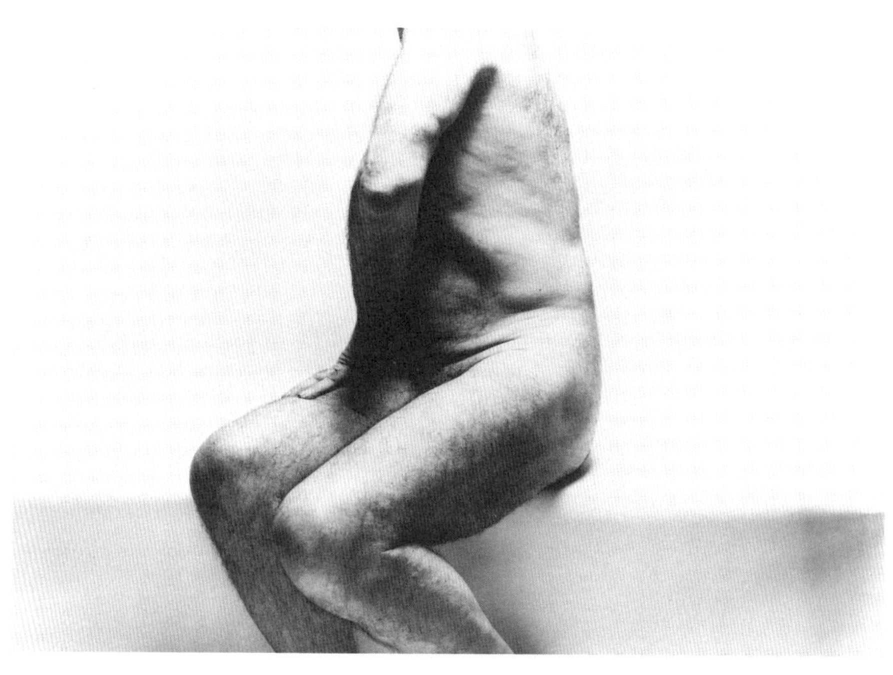

John Coplans

Seated Figure, no. 4, 1987

"THE NUDE THAT DARLING OF THE ARTISTS, THAT NECESSARY ELEMENT OF SUCCESS"[1] — DAVID MCCARTHY

MORE THAN A CENTURY AND A HALF LATER, Charles Baudelaire's ironically heartfelt assertion that the nude was just as necessary a subject then as it had been in antiquity still rings true. That most overworked of subjects continues to have a firm and important place in contemporary art. Whether avidly pursued by countless numbers of Sunday painters, diligently studied in art history surveys, mastered ad nauseam in life drawing classes, painted, sculpted, photographed or performed in a seemingly endless variety of styles, the nude refuses to go gently into that good night of irrelevance and oblivion.

Baudelaire's attention to the nude in 1846, like his attempt to define the beautiful for his time, was part of an argument concerning the heroism of modern life. Before attempting to describe the epic aspects of Parisian life, he first had to theorize the aesthetic category of the beautiful to prove that it found a home in the modern world. According to the poet and critic, beauty was a combination of the eternal and the transitory, or, as then contemporary audiences would have understood, of the classical and the modern. As he wrote,

All forms of beauty, like all possible phenomena, contain an element of the eternal and an element of the transitory—of the absolute and of the particular. Absolute and eternal beauty does not exist, or rather it is only an abstraction skimmed from the general surface of different beauties. The particular element in each manifestation comes from the emotions: and just as we have our own particular emotions, so we have our own beauty.[2]

Baudelaire's great insight was that each age found its own definition of the beautiful, which was dependent on the emotional tenor of the times. In drawing attention to the nude in this generative essay, he suggested that it too was a subject of contemporary relevance. The nude was just as important for the moment of the 1840s as it had been in the classical age because it participated in the ongoing redefinition of beauty.

Furthermore, Baudelaire argued that the nude could thrive in the modern world because "the themes and resources of painting are … abundant and varied."[3] His emphasis on plenitude and variety indicated that this traditional subject could survive and flourish if artists considered carefully where it appeared. Baudelaire mentioned the bedroom and bath, as well as the anatomy theater. None of these spaces was necessarily new, but each could reveal modern men and women as they lived in the middle decades of the nineteenth century. With great confidence he concluded that the nude was "just as frequent and necessary today as it was in the life of the ancients."[4]

As will become clear from this brief essay, and from reviewing the works in *The Nude in Contemporary Art*, the nude continues to be as abundant and as varied today as it was when Baudelaire first wrote about the heroism of modern life. As will become equally clear, the nude can carry almost any meaning and content that artists decide to ascribe to it in the late twentieth century. Paradoxically, the nude is both overflowing with the history that

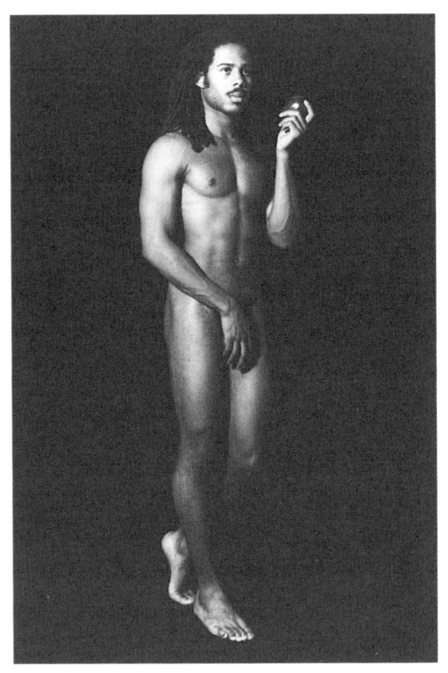

Renée Cox

Adam, 1995

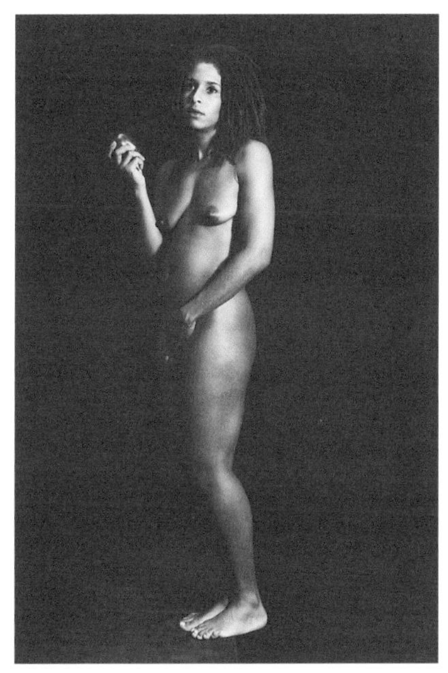

Renée Cox

Eve, 1995

precedes it, and constantly waiting to be reanimated by the concerns of artists in the present. Baudelaire noted that the transitory and the particular are evident in the beautiful (of which the nude is an example), which is one reason this ancient subject continues to hold our attention. Like Narcissus gazing intently at his own reflection, our consideration of the nude might reflect back to us the unique tenor of our times.

Given the historical origins of the nude, any consideration of the subject requires a look at previous times and places. By looking backward we can begin to appreciate the complexity of our moment. Such an exercise is both salutary and sobering because it will reveal just how indebted we are to previous artists and ideas, while also clarifying, and perhaps explaining, the concerns of the present.

A Classical Model

In his memorable definition of the nude, the British art historian Kenneth Clark claimed that it was "a balanced, prosperous, and confident body: the body re-formed."[5] His insight was

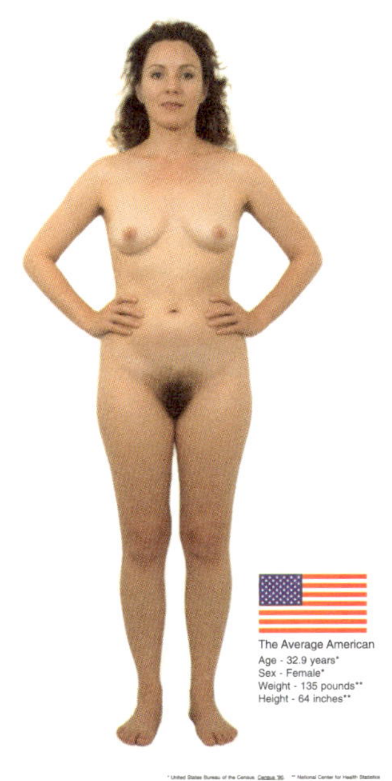

Meg Cranston

The Average American, 1996

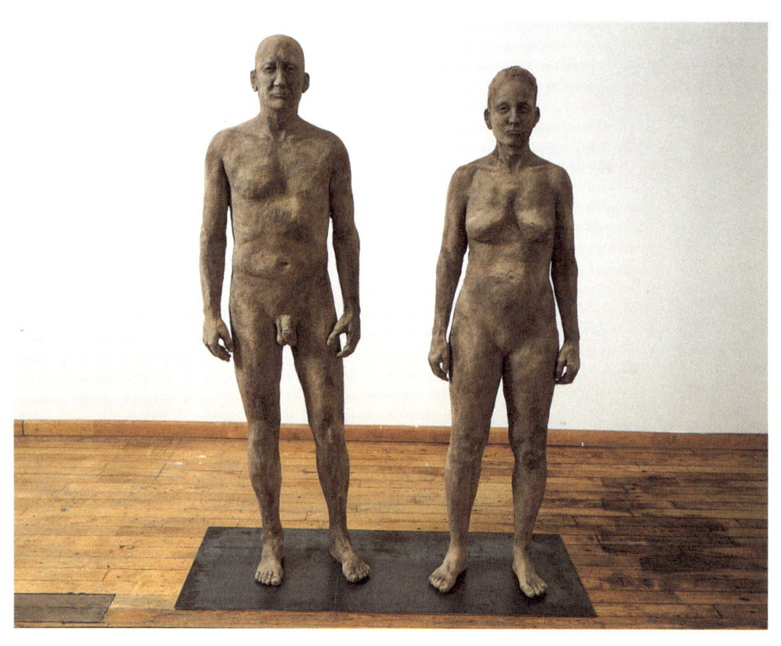

James Croak

Man and Woman, 1998

based on a careful review of eighteenth-century art criticism that identified the example of classical art as the fitting precedent and justification for the subject. The nude was not just any body, but the human body reconfigured according to accepted standards of proportion and decorum. It was the body cleaned up, transformed, and elevated into an ideal. In short, the nude was a form of art, and perhaps even "the central subject of art" as Clark asserted.[6] In distinction, actual bodies were deemed "the naked," which implied that they were not yet dressed up to play a part in the heroic narratives of Greek history and mythology. By grounding his definition in classical examples, Clark rightly intimated that the nude was a retrospective subject that took its authority from the founding moment of Western art. Almost without fail, all subsequent nudes, regardless of where they fall in the continuum between the nude and the naked, are produced with a keen awareness of antique prototypes.

Two stories handed down from the classical period haunt the subject, and reveal the tension between an ideal and the real, as well as the extent to which the nude is a projection of fantasy and sometimes frustration. In Ovid's *Metamorphosis*, the sculptor Pygmalion crafted his image of female perfection because he abhorred the "many faults which nature has implanted in the female sex."[7] Working with ivory, he sculpted his ideal.

Later, praying to the goddess Venus, he intimated that he wished her to come to life. His kiss transformed her cold, inert form into the warm and pliable substance of actual flesh. This impossible moment is captured in Jean-Léon Gérôme's academic painting, *Pygmalion and Galatea* (ca. 1881, Metropolitan Museum of Art), in which her flesh is gradually succumbing to the warm embrace of her creator / lover. The metaphor of artists transforming their materials into the magical realm of art is here conjoined with the desire to find a living embodiment of one's fantasy.

The second story that stands behind the classical nude comes from the Roman scholar Pliny the Elder.[8] In his chapters on the history of art, he recounted a particularly difficult public art commission. The painter Zeuxis was hired to produce a portrait of Hera for a temple in Agrigentum. Believing that no single mortal woman could serve as the model for the wife of Zeus, he had several local young women stripped for his inspection. He then took the most perfect parts of some, but not all, of the women before him, and recombined them into a whole. If the story sounds something like our modern beauty pageants with women willingly stripping down to engage the critical eyes of a male judge, it should. In its historical formation, the nude was a reminder that beauty was competitive, and that it conformed to a conceptual ideal.

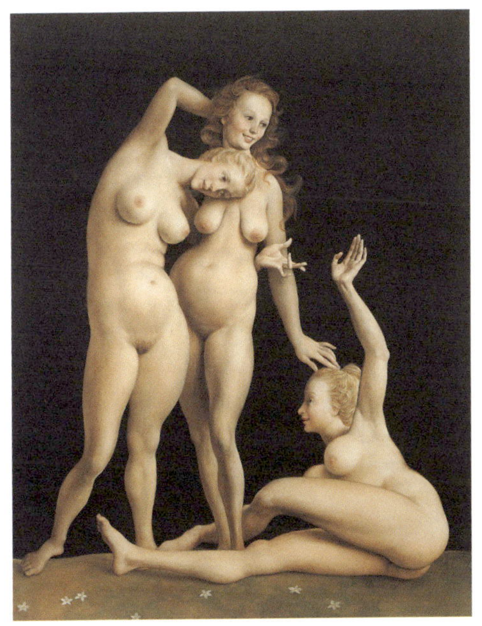

John Currin

Three Friends, 1998

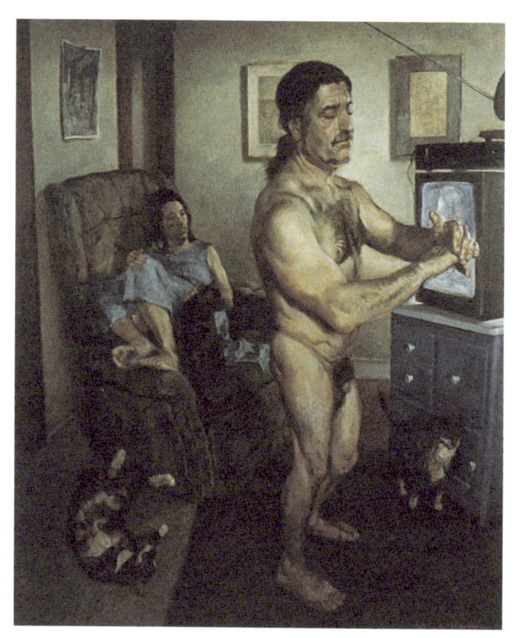

Steven DiGiovanni

Coin Toss, 1998

A review of female and male nudes in classical art bears out the importance of these lasting stories and of Clark's definition. Whether we turn to the solitary, standing kore and kouros figures from the sixth century, or to the sculptural groups on various temple pediments in subsequent centuries, we are constantly confronted with images of perfection. By this standard of measure, the nude stands above the variety of natural forms. It is a reminder that art, in its classical formation at least, is an improvement on nature itself.

We also need to remember that the nude often had an allegorical function. It could connote innocence, truth, and vulnerability, as well as vanity, enticement and desire. Therefore the nude is not only a subject within Western art, but also it is a form of communication within visual language. Knowing this, we have to ask whether any given nude represents a specific person, humanity in general, or perhaps an emotion or abstraction. Depending on the additional information with which artists surround it, the nude can stand for the beautiful or the grotesque, desire or repulsion, the embodied or the eternal, and the concrete or the abstract. How we read specific nudes will thus depend on the historical examples we identify, as well as the subjects they illustrate.

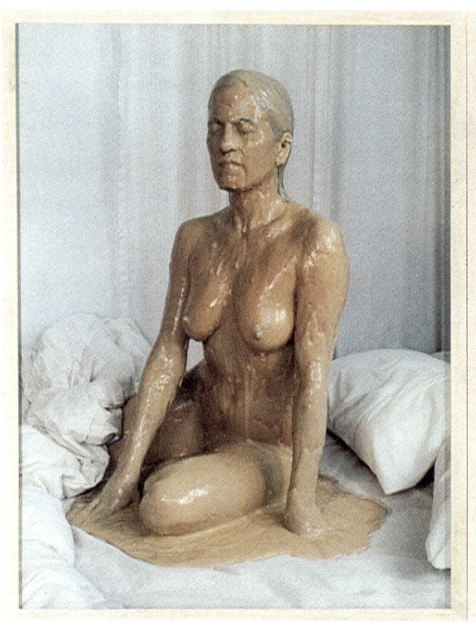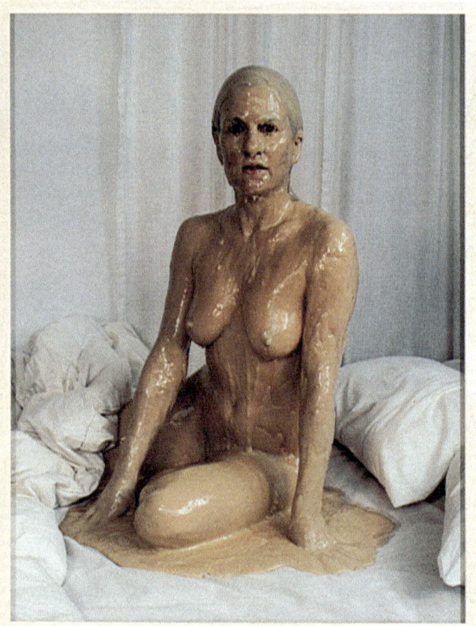

Jeanne Dunning

Puddle I, 1997

For several centuries the nude has been an inescapable part of studio practice. Karen Finley's performance/installation, *Go Figure,* is a timely reminder that the nude is frequently inseparable from institutionalized education, whether sponsored by art centers, museums or universities. Since the founding of art academies in the sixteenth century, drawing from life has been a staple of art education. Before moving on to the more taxing challenge of organizing historical and religious subjects, students were expected to demonstrate their competence in delineating accurately the human body. Like Zeuxis and Pygmalion in earlier centuries, art students were trained to edit and improve upon the bodies of models so that they might conform to the ideal of classical art. Typically, the life drawing studio contained plaster casts of antique sculpture. While drawing from the figure, one could seek inspiration and guidance from the appropriate models of previous art. An aquatint by Thomas Rowlandson and Augustus Barry Pugin in The Metropolitan Museum of Art clearly illustrates the rigors of life drawing, and reminds us that despite its sometimes erotic content, the nude is always the product of labor.

Rowlandson and Pugin's illustration of a life drawing class nearly two centuries ago also reminds us that the subject is often based on a profound awareness of historical

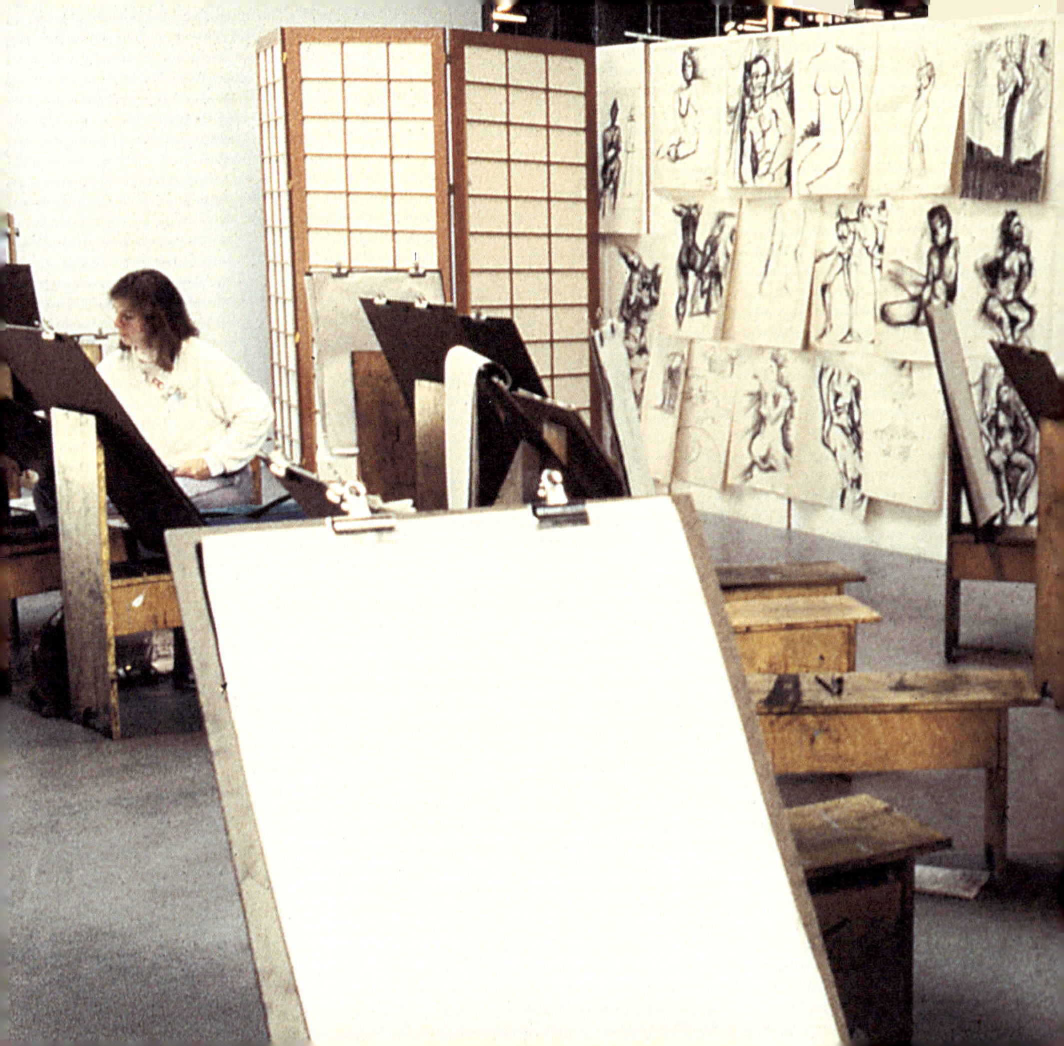

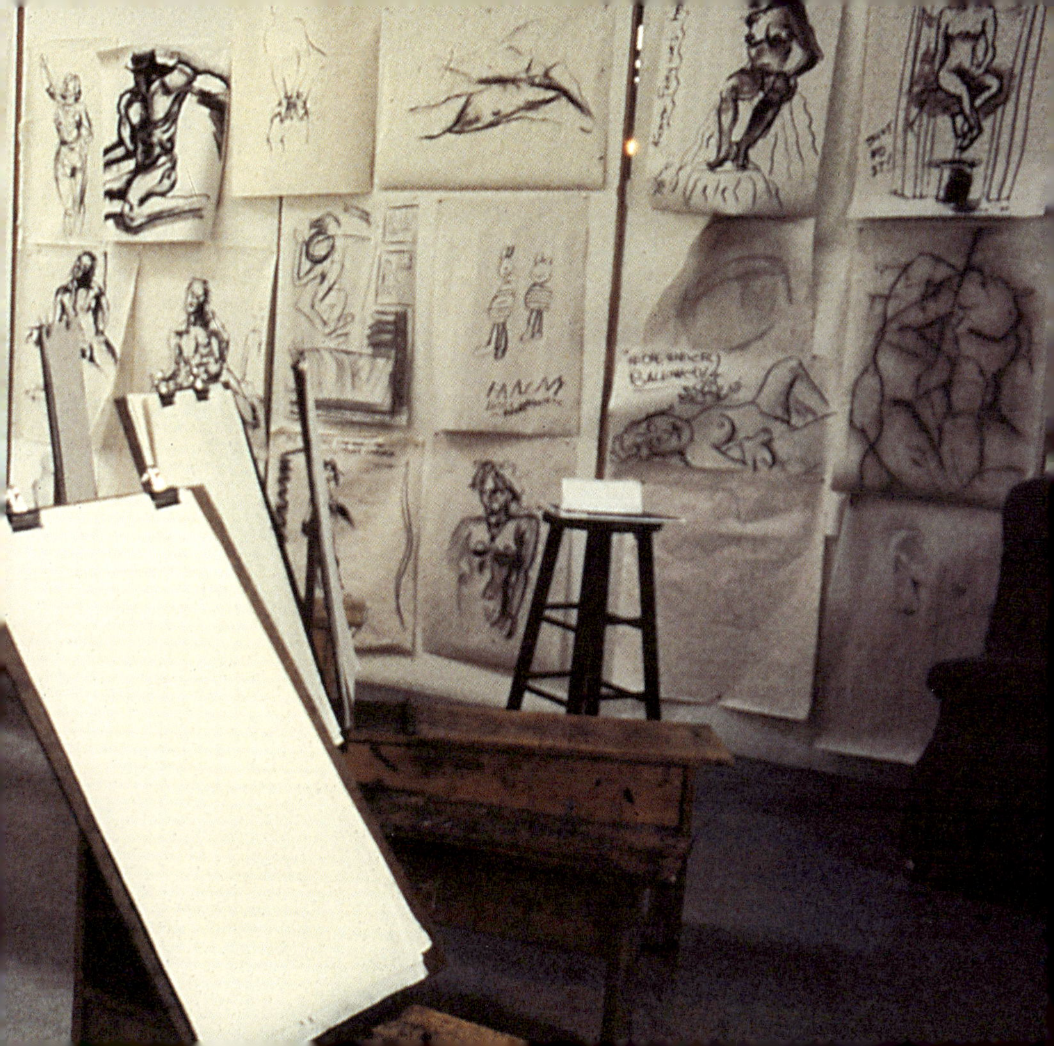

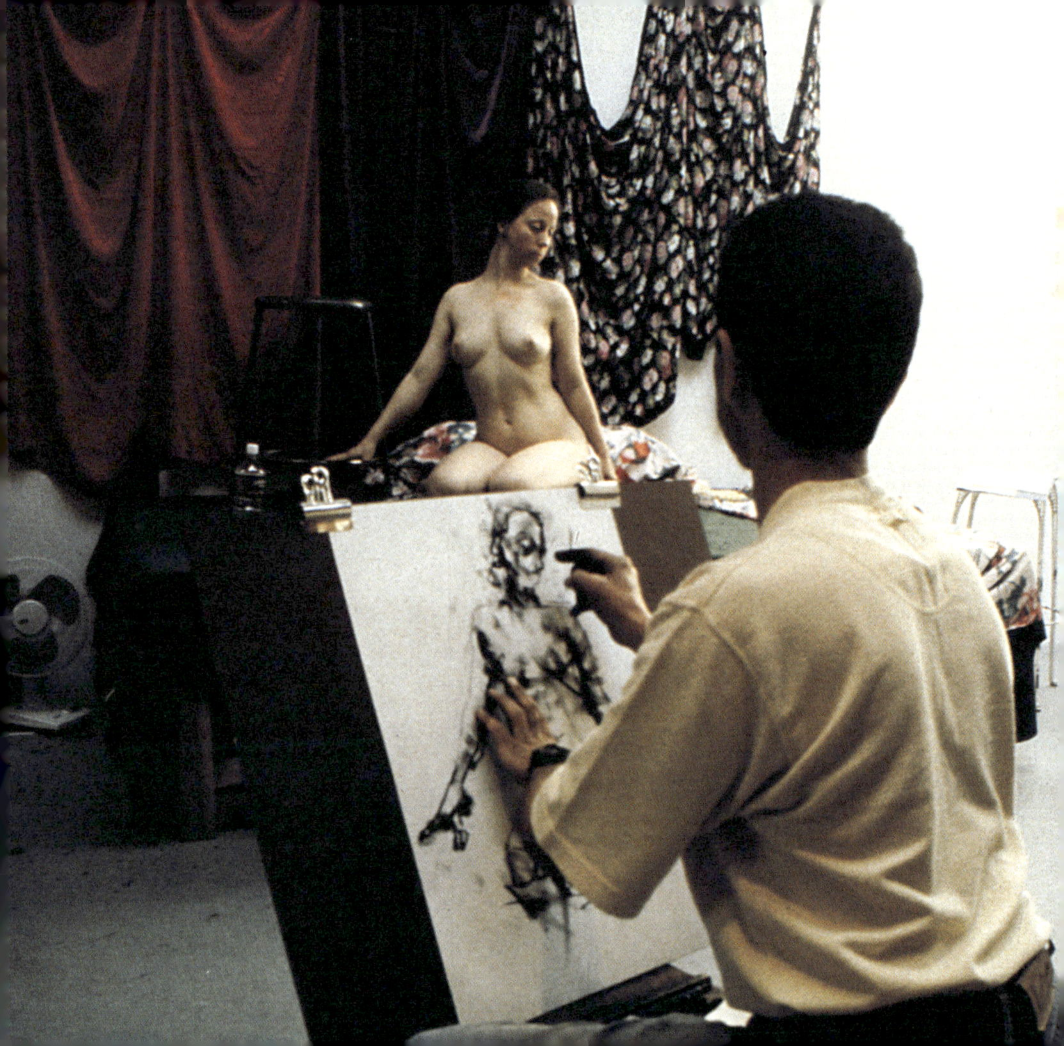

precedent. Almost without exception we can identify a source of inspiration for any nude. For example, Edouard Manet's scandalous painting of a prostitute, *Olympia* (1863, Musée d' Orsay, Paris), is clearly based on Titian's canonical *Venus of Urbino* (ca. 1534, Galleria degli Uffizi, Florence), which in turn invokes the legacy of a common ancient subject, the *Venus Pudica*, or modest Venus who vainly attempts to cover her breasts and genitals from the prying eyes of interested spectators. Clearly, education is necessary for producing nudes and for appreciating them too. Knowing this, we might conclude that the subject, in addition to its potential for erotic stimulation, is an exercise in historical thinking whereby contemporary artists recognize the authority of previous art.

If the nude is often retrospective, it is also a source of challenge. As much as it forces artists to look over their shoulders to acknowledge what has come before, the nude also induces a strongly reflective process. Reflection can imply passive mirroring, whether copying the mass of a model's body faithfully or working within an established convention, such as the reclining female nude or the active standing male nude. But reflection can also involve an intensely active element of processing. In producing a parody of Titian's *Venus of Urbino*, Manet faced several daunting questions: how might he contribute to an ongoing history? what could

Pages 56 – 58: Karen Finley

Go Figure, MoCA at the Geffen Contemporary, 1997

he do to surpass Titian's example? how could he make Titian seem outdated without fully dismissing his important example? how might Manet's nude relate to the moment of the 1860s? and why would he wish to make his reputation with such a seemingly hackneyed subject? The fact that so many nudes are banal, and have been for several centuries, is an indication of how difficult the subject remains.

Additionally, the nude, unlike still life or landscape, must pass the rigorous judgment of verisimilitude. Does it render the human body accurately or at least expressively, not to mention aesthetically? When poorly drawn it reveals the artist's failed apprenticeship in life drawing. If it cannot cohere as a moving composition it remains mere illustration. As Picasso and other modern artists demonstrated early in this century, the subject can stand a considerable degree of distortion and fragmentation. However, in the hands of lesser artists, the nude is too often lazy shorthand for art in general, and therefore is hardly worth looking at twice.

Clearly we can begin to see that the nude is a test for artists, no matter at what stage of their careers, because it reduces them to the status of students assimilating the history of Western art. The nude is also a test of their skill in rendering or capturing human

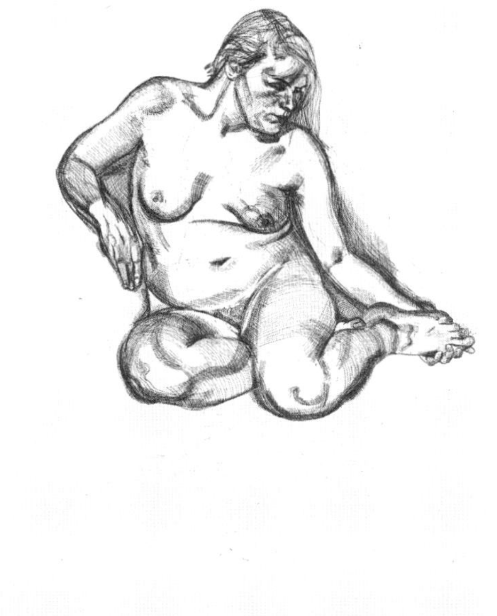

Lucian Freud

Girl Holding Her Foot, 1985

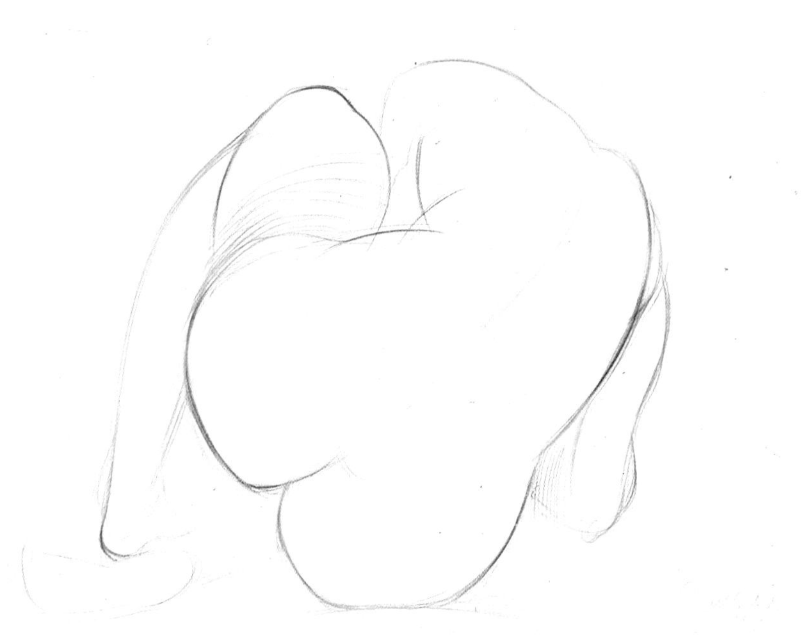

Philip Grausman

Figure Study, 1996

anatomy. For spectators, in turn, the nude is a test of one's education. Can we recognize the precedents well enough to judge the relative success and failure of each work before us? Can we discern the allusions to previous art, while also recognizing how this particular body might lead into the areas of the transitory, the particular, and the emotional identified by Baudelaire?

A Modern Subject

In the decades following Baudelaire's suggestion that the nude was a necessary subject in contemporary art, many painters and photographers produced nudes that broke with classical precedent. As academic art gradually lost its hold on the imaginations of ambitious, vanguard artists, the nude was unhinged from its ideal prototypes to take on the lineaments of contemporary life. Confronted by the recent development of photography and the efflorescence of printed materials, both of which were sometimes pornographic, the classical nude no longer seemed germane to the modern world. In subsequent decades, artists would be able to identify several precedents, from the classical to the realist, as they made this ancient subject into one that was thoroughly modern. Arguably, this modernization continues nearly unabated into the present.

Throughout the 1850s and 1860s, Gustave Courbet expanded the boundaries traditionally constraining the nude. His painting *The Bathers* (1853, Musée Fabre, Montpellier) placed a corpulent female nude with a servant dressed in contemporary garb near a stream. At once invoking the legacy of classical nymphs in the landscape or of ladies at their bath, the painting also asserted that within realist discourse the body must betray the sag and weight of actual flesh. Hardly ideal, Courbet's nude was a parody of academic art and a call to break with convention. Contemporary critics were both appalled and fascinated; some suggested that the unnerving power of this nude was its revelation of an unwashed, lower-class body.[9] If such readings were a projection of social tensions, they nonetheless demonstrate, as Baudelaire intimated, that the modern nude would betray the emotional tenor of its time.

The desire to forsake classical conventions of proportion and presentation was a legacy Courbet bequeathed to later artists. His ungainly women were invoked by Pablo Picasso in late 1906 as he began to ridicule the conventional prettiness of the female nude. Within a year he would turn to African artifacts with their conceptual simplifications

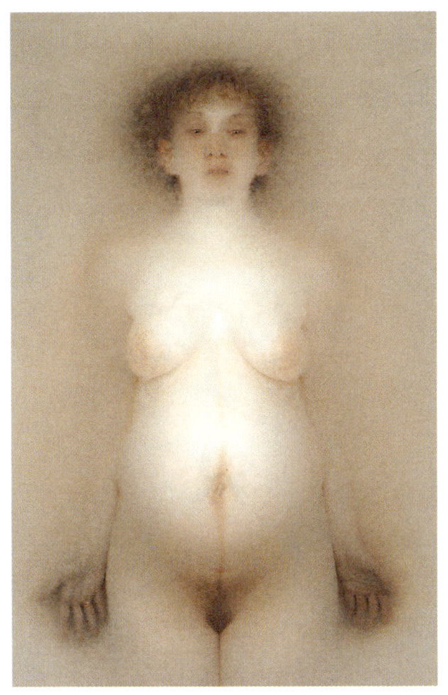

Anne Harris

Third Portrait with Max, 1996–97

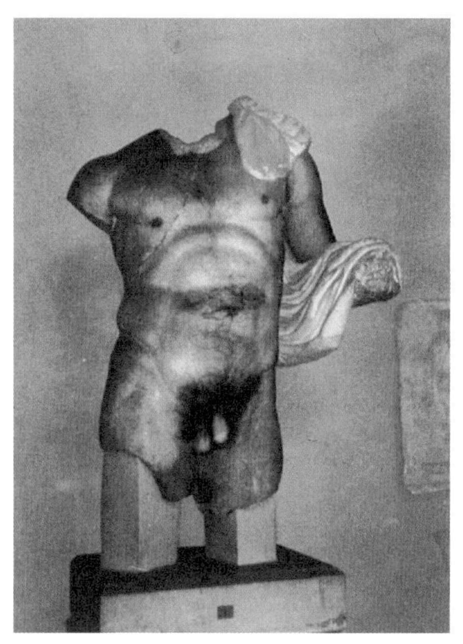

Jacqueline Hayden

Ancient Statuary Series # 2, 1997

and distortions of the human body in his signature work, *Les Demoiselles d'Avignon* (1907, The Museum of Modern Art, New York), which placed five undressed women in a brothel. Some fifty years later Larry Rivers deliberately invoked Courbet's women in a famous portrait nude of his aging, corpulent mother-in-law, *Double Portrait of Berdie* (1955, Whitney Museum of American Art, New York). In the current exhibition, Laura Aguilar, Sherry Camhy, and Hanneline Røgeberg continue the realist emphasis on recording bodies as they are.

More importantly, Courbet's nudes established a precedent whereby subsequent artists would announce their ambition and public arrival by painting a nude. Manet made his reputation with two paintings featuring nudes, the *Déjeuner sur l'herbe* (Musée d'Orsay, Paris) and *Olympia*, shown at the Salon des Refusés (1863) and Paris Salon of 1865 respectively. Cézanne would soon follow with a series of parodies, and would continue to produce paintings of nudes, mostly classicizing, until his death in 1907. In the same year Picasso made his canonical *Les Demoiselles d'Avignon*, which by some historical accounts stands as the entryway to subsequent vanguard art in the twentieth century.

Indeed, in the nearly fifty years separating Manet's famous paintings and the outbreak of World War I, the nude would figure in the work of many vanguard artists, all of whom recognized that the subject was ideally situated to touch on the most interesting and stimulating concerns of the moment, from prostitution and venereal disease to the sexual behavior of non-Western individuals. For Picasso and Matisse, the nude was a constant test of their creative powers. They produced nudes well into the twentieth century, often in awareness of one another, and frequently in competition with the masterpieces of Western art.[10] Almost without fail, we can see a continuous history from Courbet and Manet in the middle of the nineteenth century, to Picasso and Willem de Kooning a hundred years later, in which the female nude was considered a subject of serious challenge.

Controversy

Over the past decade we have witnessed several challenges to the autonomy of artists whose use of the human body some audiences found deeply offensive. Robert Mapplethorpe's gorgeous photographs of idealized men (sometimes engaged in sexual acts unknown to many Americans), like Karen Finley's performances using her own body and edible solids, challenged

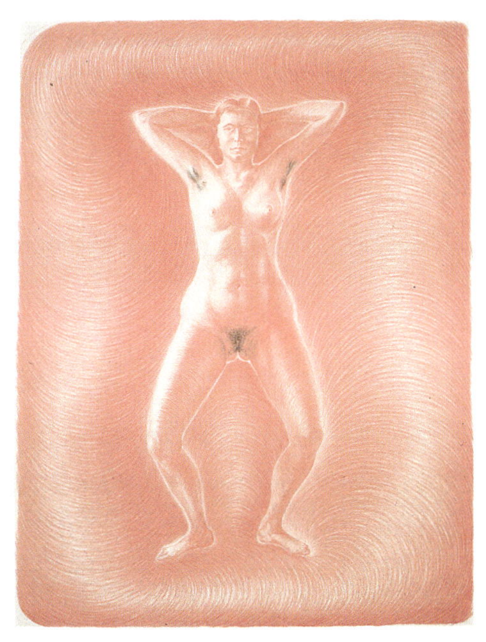

Kinke Kooi

Hairy Woman, 1992

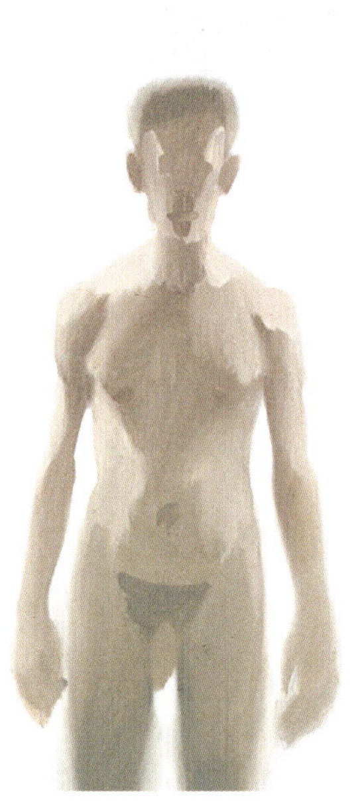

Peter Krashes

Untitled Series #3, 1996

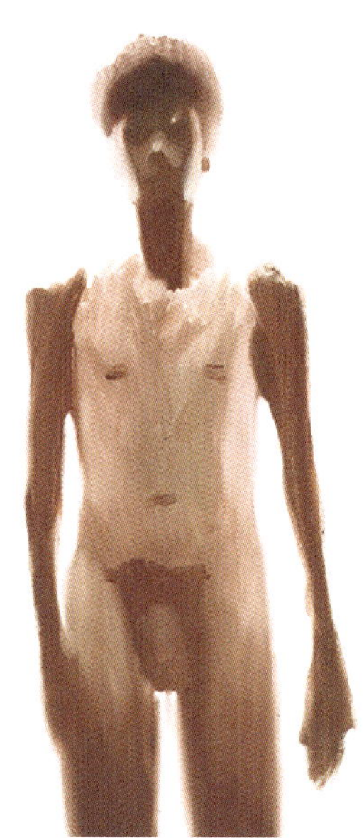

Peter Krashes

Untitled Series #1, 1996

traditional definitions of what the body could do in public spaces, and how it should be contained by mainstream mores. If on one hand their art seems to be a far remove from the often chaste and genteel conventions of the nude, on the other hand it should remind us that controversy is less a function of the art itself than it is a projection from audiences who feel challenged or threatened by imagery they find objectionable.

What constitutes the objectionable, however, is often a function of personal taste, which in turn is affected by religious affiliation, educational background, economic status, sexual identity, and all of the other variables that contribute to human subjectivity. Consider the following diatribe:

You enter [the Uffizi], and proceed to that most-visited little gallery that exists in the world — the Tribune — and there, against the wall, without obstructing rag or leaf, you may look your fill upon the foulest, the vilest, the obscenest picture the world possesses — Titian's Venus.[11]

Although better known as a novelist and wit than as an art critic, the author was no simpleton or rube, and we would be remiss to castigate him too severely for attacking Titian's masterpiece.

Mark Twain's objection centered on the placement and potential activity of Venus's left hand. To the American author, it suggested "impure" thoughts, as Mapplethorpe's photographs would to several senators over a century later. But as the author realized then, Titian's Venus had every right to recline languidly in an art gallery, "for she is a work of art, and Art has its privileges."[12]

Some of those privileges extend to the viewing public, and include looking avidly at the undressed human body. Perhaps we might suggest that the activity of walking through an art gallery gazing at the sometimes ideal and sometimes real bodies of humans is supposed to be different from surreptitiously scanning back issues of *National Geographic* in the dentist's office when we were children, or furtively groping for the centerfold of a *Playboy* in adolescence. And one would hope that a work of art provides experiences and insights not available in documentary photography or soft-core pornography. However, a firm historical function of the nude, dating back to the fertility figurines of prehistory, is to arouse sexual desire.

Yet as we now know after several decades of attention to human sexuality, desire is mutable and varied. Part of the traditional tension found within the nude in the past two centuries is the revelation of anatomical and sexual difference. Ideals vary across

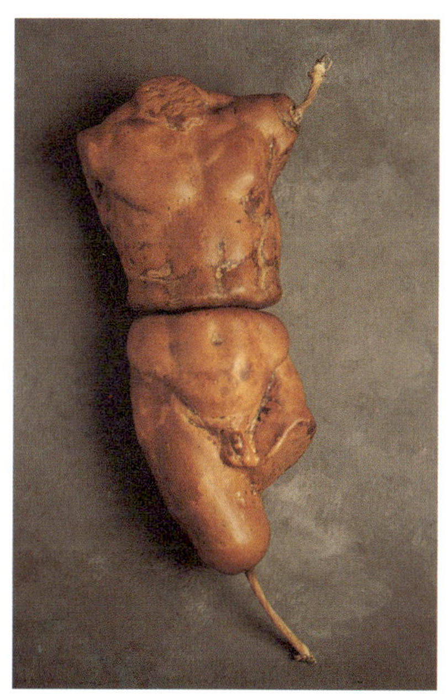

Daniel Ladd

Silenus (reduction and fragment), 1998

Attributed to Lysippos, 3rd Century B.C., Vatican Museum

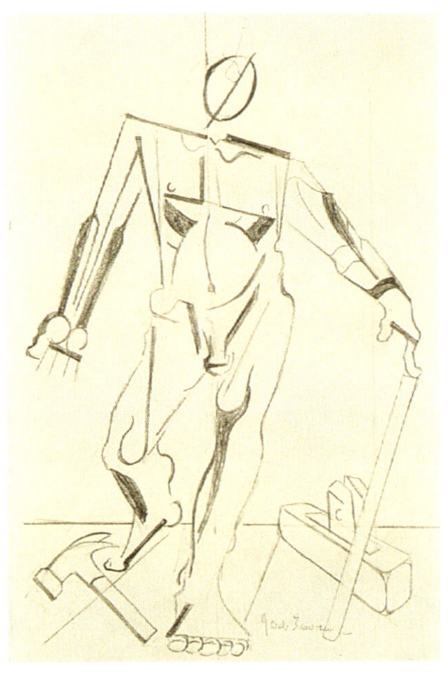

Jacob Lawrence

Standing man with Hammer and Plane, 1996

time and place, as Baudelaire argued in the 1840s and as Courbet demonstrated a decade later. Questions of propriety also vary, as Mark Twain's prudish objection to Titian's Venus reveals. If the nude remains occasionally controversial, this is so because it provides a convenient, visible, and often public target for addressing the human body as a locus of erotic desire, no matter how that desire may be construed.

The Perpetual Present

Over the past fifty years artists around the world have turned to the nude in a variety of media, in the process wedding this most traditional of subjects to the heroism of modern life. In part the postwar interest in the nude is understandable as a rejection of abstraction in modern painting and sculpture. The nude provided artists with the opportunity to work with recognizable subject matter. More importantly, the nude allowed artists to tie themselves to an ongoing tradition while also examining the dramatic changes in society that placed the body, its pleasures and experiences, at the very center of human consciousness. Although this

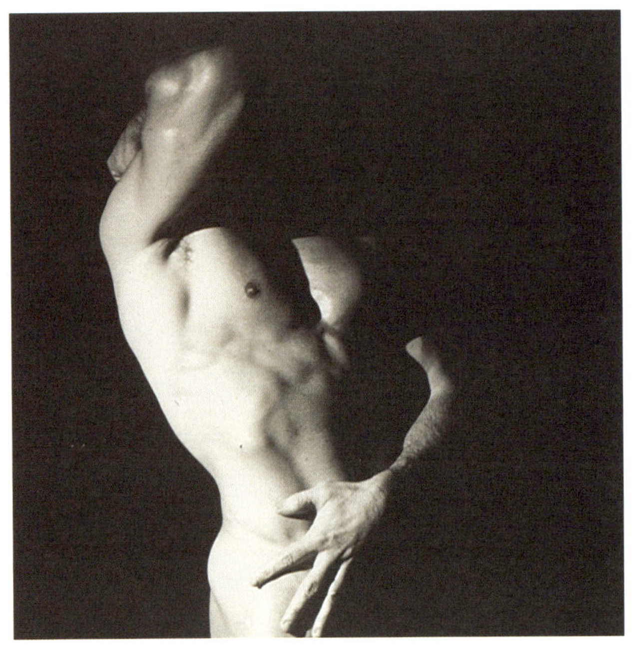

Harriet Leibowitz

Larry I, 1995

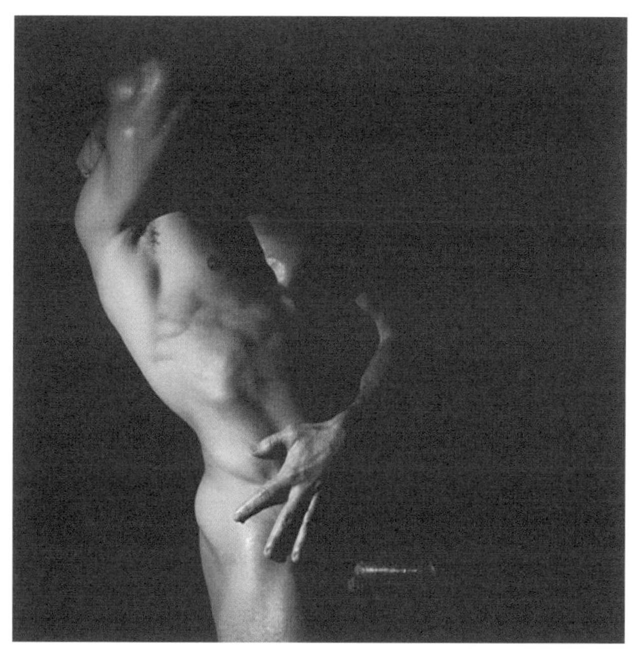

Harriet Leibowitz

Larry II, 1995

sometimes made for confrontational and controversial art, it also provided a public forum through which society could discuss its most immediate concerns.

The democratizing impulse that surged through the visual arts in the sixties helped transform the nude into a subject of youthful exploration. Young and old artists alike found that the body was both topical and challenging. By focusing on the nude, or on the undressed body in general, many artists could use the theme as a convenient peg upon which to hang virtually any issue then in vogue. The youth revolution was often signified by undressed bodies, as was protest against the war in Vietnam. Black, feminist, and gay consciousness raising often included nudes, because the subject both attracted immediate attention and registered the nuances of identity politics. This growing attention to ethnicity and race, not to mention the noisy public discourses of gender and sexuality, affected the look of the contemporary body. With an increasingly heterogeneous audience, the nude is rapidly becoming all things to all people. Instead of one, classically-derived ideal, we now have several, which substantiates Baudelaire's call for modern beauty.

Perhaps most important for the decades of the sixties and seventies, and those that followed, was the feminist emphasis on making the personal political. How women

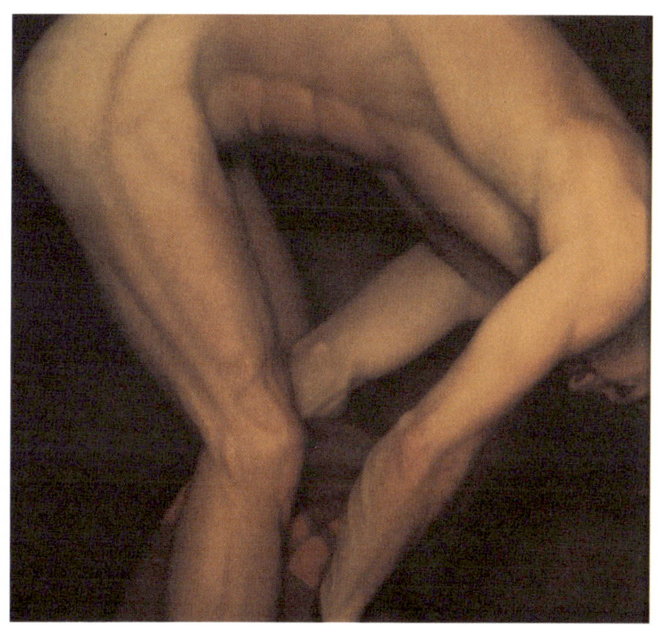

Michael Leonard

Male Bather, 1989

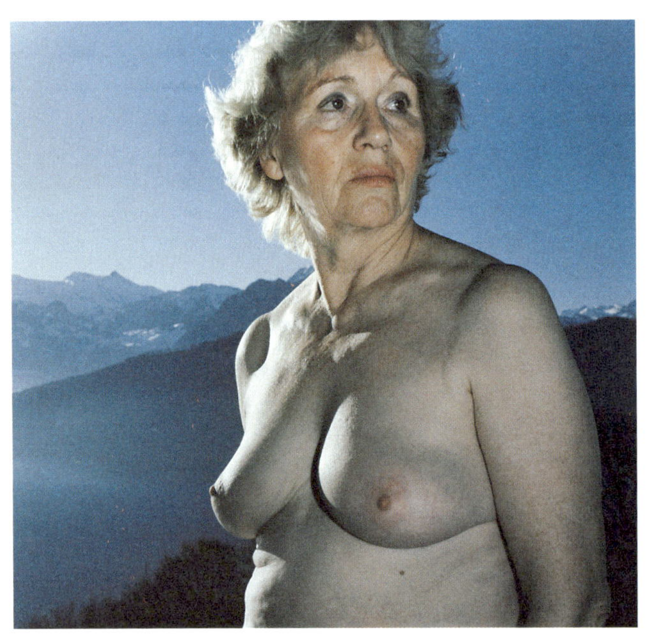

Melanie Manchot

With Mountains I, 1999

lived in their bodies, how they could talk about their bodies, and how their libidinal drives were understood, were issues inseparable from broader questions of access to power within society as a whole. As it quickly became apparent, the feminist re-examination of the nude in painting, photography, and performance art was tied to this general ferment. Where in years past the nude too often was subordinate to male, heterosexual fantasy, under the impact of feminism, the nude, whether female or male, suddenly became the sign of alternative experiences and desires. Added to this was a keen awareness of the extent to which mass media, advertising, pornography—and even art—perpetuated sexist stereotypes. By making the female body in general, and their bodies in particular, a central concern within feminist discourse, artists such as Joan Semmel, Carolee Schneemann, Sylvia Sleigh, and Hannah Wilke, helped transform the nude from a thorny, sometimes offensive, subject into a powerful vehicle for addressing the experiences of women.

In the nineties, several women continue to make self-portrait nudes that examine personal experience. Anne Harris's depictions of her pregnancy record the natural, yet dramatic transformation of the female body as it carries a fetus to term. Laura Aguilar's *Nature Self-Portraits* celebrate abundant flesh while perpetuating the old trope of likening the female body to the earth, perhaps most famously explored by Ana Mendieta twenty years ago. Denise Marika's video installation stages an ambiguous physical encounter with her husband in which her nudity signifies honesty, truth, vulnerability, and desirability. All are traditionally associated with the female nude, but here are given an immediacy through Marika's willingness to bring them to life through performance.

Throughout the sixties and seventies Philip Pearlstein and other New Realist painters systematically avoided the classical and erotic connotations of the nude. Believing that the subject was too often sentimental and hackneyed, they approached it as a formal exercise in arranging shape, line and color on a two-dimensional surface. If their results seemed anti-romantic, their paintings nonetheless brought a conceptual rigor to the topic, which helped revive the realist emphasis on specific bodies in actual spaces first introduced by Gustave Courbet in the 1850s.

The realist emphasis on everyday bodies provides an ongoing model for keeping the nude current. Tina Barney's disarmingly banal photographs of models seated and walking through the living spaces of Manhattan apartments demonstrate that the subject can find its exoticism in the most common of spaces. Harriet Casdin-Silver's hologram,

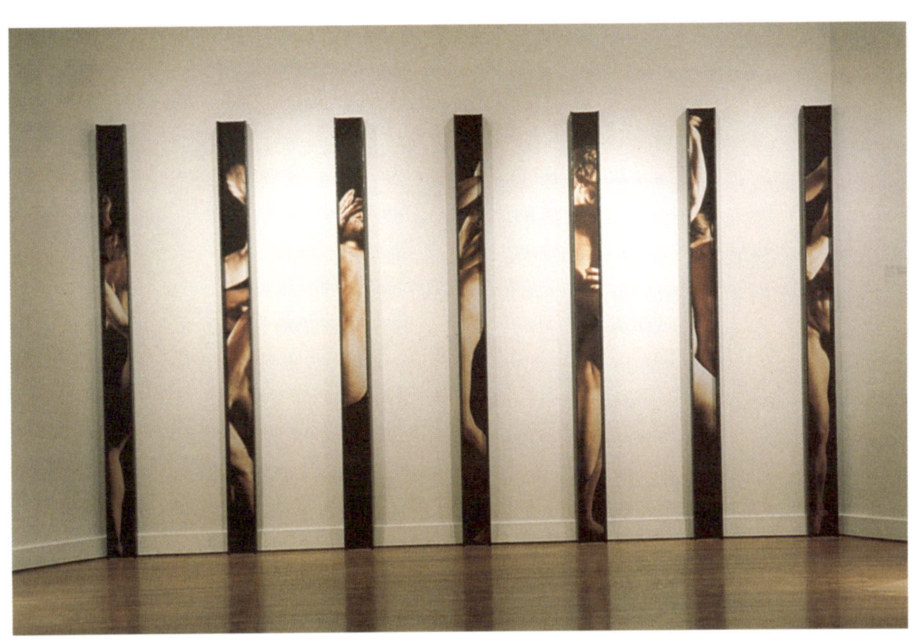

Denise Marika

Battle, 1994–1995

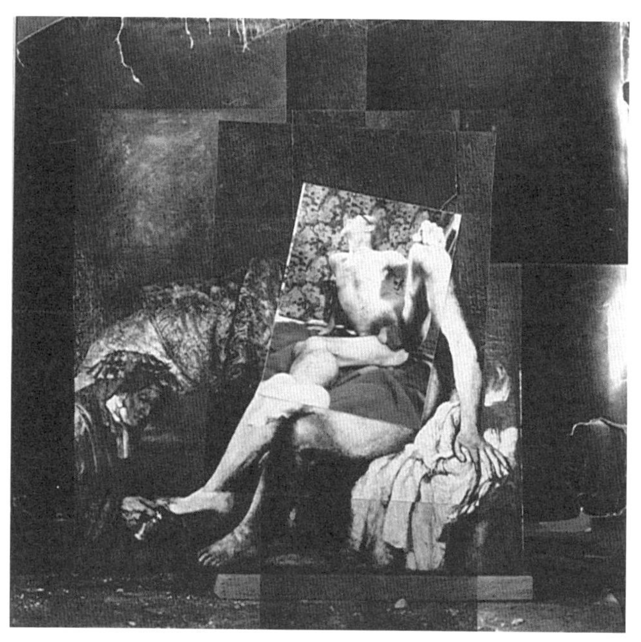

John O'Reilly

Dutch Bedroom, 1997

To Soutine and Matisse, introduces a degree of verisimilitude that encourages us to suspend our disbelief and accept, if only momentarily, that the bodies before us are real. Even when these bodies disappear as we shift our physical position before the hologram, they provide an abrupt reminder that the distance between the nude as a convention and the body as we live in it is quite tangible.

Uniting feminists and realists alike, with the two camps often overlapping, was a keen awareness of how the human body was shaped through mass media. Both groups were opposed to the staged eroticism and fanciful idealism of pornography. For feminists the pornographic was too often a means of objectifying and subordinating women, forcing their sexualities to coincide with those of straight men. For realists, the airbrushed bodies of Playmates had little to do with the rich variety of actual human bodies. Advertising too perpetuates impossibly ideal stereotypes, particularly in its presentation of women. The long, slender bodies of many models, whether thirty years ago or today, fit a set of proportions that few actual women can claim naturally. When the nude in contemporary art rejects such ideals, we can see it as a form of resistance and a confirmation of individual variety.

Not only does the nude come in all shapes and sizes, but also it continues to be identified with many different, and often traditional, subjects. When placed at water's edge or in verdant fields, it evokes the tradition of arcadianism, of the peaceful union between humans and nature. Cézanne and Matisse explored such terrain early in this century; Jock Sturges's photographs of nude bathers demonstrate that the theme is very much alive in the 1990s. In the studio the nude suggests the quiet meditation of artists carefully manipulating their materials to translate the body into the languages of sculpture, painting, and photography. The theme occupied Thomas Eakins last century, and appears in collages by John O'Reilly. An undressed body in the living room, kitchen, or bathroom can evoke the intimacy of shared family spaces, as is evident in Steven DiGiovanni's marvelously mundane *Coin Toss*.

Variety, as Baudelaire intimated, was a means of capturing the tenor of the present. The sheer range of possibilities for depicting the nude, no matter how defined, is one reason the subject has not disappeared. Although the undressed body remains a stable subject, the spaces surrounding it, as well as the other objects in that space, are constantly being updated. Moreover, the body itself is historically determined, which is to say it is perpetually revised. Zeuxis's ideal was as much a product of its moment as Meg Cranston's *The Average*

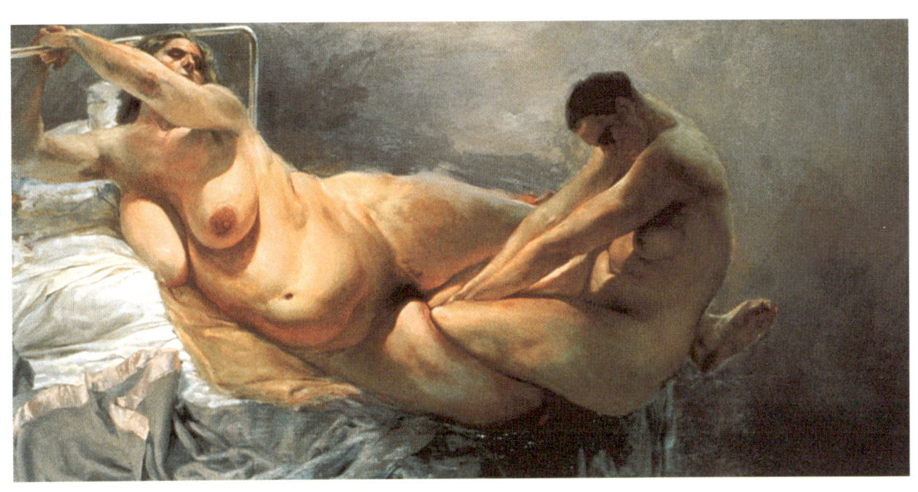

Hanneline Røgeberg

Ex-It, 1995

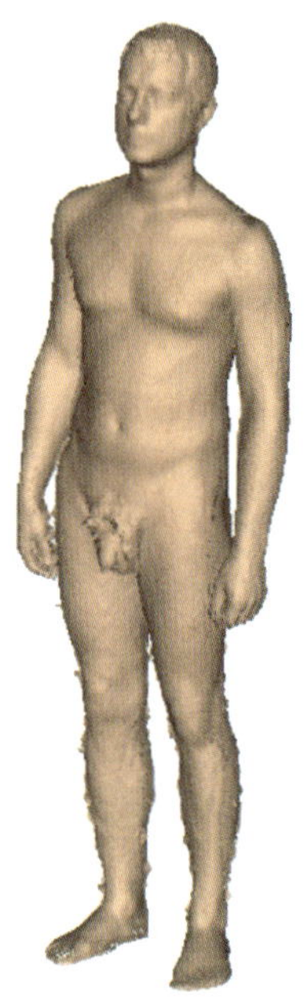

Karin Sander

Clemens 1:5 (raw data), 1999

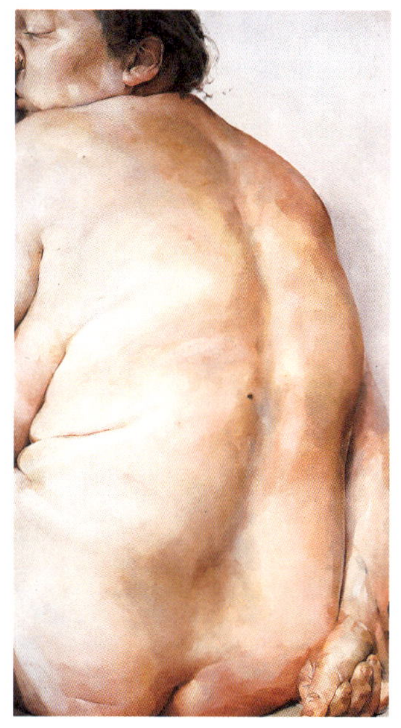

Jenny Saville

Untitled, 1994

American is of our time. Indeed, the ideal nude is as much a temporal idea as it is an eternal one. In other words, the nude reveals exactly what and how much importance we invest in our bodies. Who we are determines how our nudes will look, while in turn our nudes reveal to us what we find important within our moment.

Given the increasing number of artists who think about the nude, we might surmise that a rich heterogeneity characterizes the current treatment of the subject. Certainly a moment that embraces such diverse media as painting, photography, video, holography, performance, and sculpture, should induce a wide range of approaches to the subject. Yet within this current situation, there are themes that cut across media and style, and that return us to the traditional challenges of the nude.

For a subject that is so readily tied to the history of art, reference and appropriation remain strong tendencies. In the early sixties Tom Wesselmann produced his *Great American Nude* series in clear homage to Matisse and Manet, while in the following decade Sylvia Sleigh parodied such masters as Velázquez, Titian, and Ingres. In the eighties and nineties John O'Reilly produced several collages that inserted his body into famous tableaux, whether atop a kouros figure from The Metropolitan Museum of Art in *Archaic Self-Portrait,*

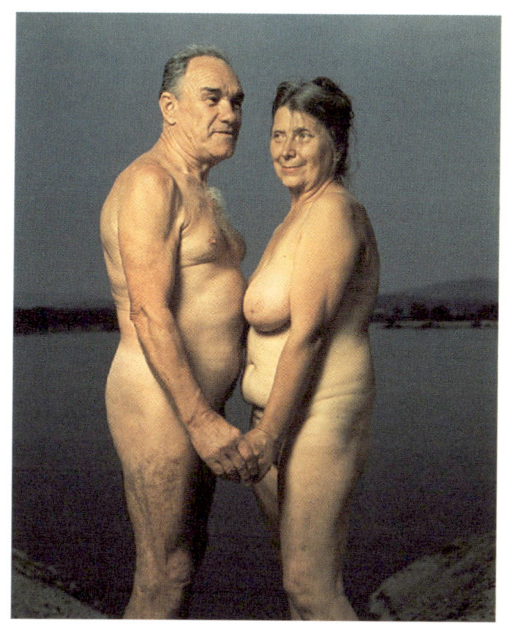

Andres Serrano

Budapest (The Lake), 1994

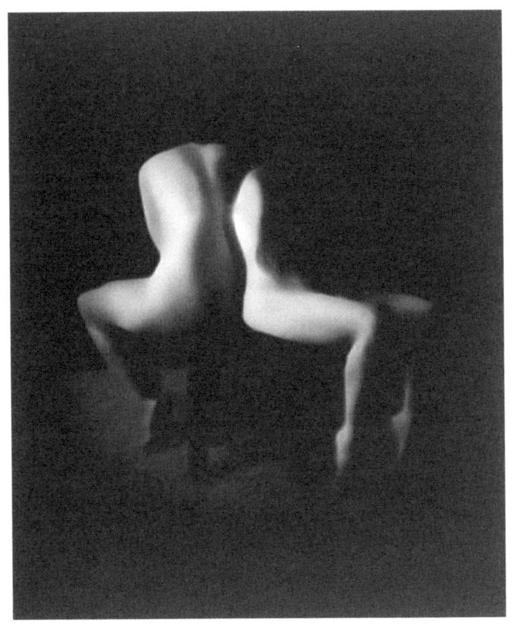

Robert Stivers

Series 5 (two figures), 1994

or inside Rembrandt's painting, *Bathsheba at Her Bath* (1654, Musée du Louvre, Paris), in the aptly titled *Dutch Bedroom*. Daniel Ladd's cast gourds mimic famous sculptures from antiquity and pre-history with vegetable matter forced to take on the shape of carved sculpture, while Jacqueline Hayden's photographs mixing actual bodies with the pedestals used to display Roman art conflate the contemporary and the ancient. John Currin's oddly organic rumination on the Three Graces invokes the alternative ideal of Northern Renaissance painting found in the work of Lucas Cranach the Elder. Clearly the nude remains firmly connected with previous approaches to the subject, suggesting that our moment in the late twentieth century is, at least in some ways, a continuation of earlier epochs.

Another theme that seems to unite many artists' thinking about the nude in recent years is the willingness to work locally with what is at hand. Historically artists often turned to themselves, their family, and their friends for models. In the fifties Larry Rivers painted portrait nudes of his best friend, the poet Frank O'Hara, as well as his ex-wife, his sons, and his mother-in-law. Today we can turn to Brett Bigbee, John Coplans, Anne Harris, Denise Marika, and John O'Reilly for keeping the subject firmly within the family. As their work demonstrates, the nude continues to be a subject by and through which we can discuss childhood and old age, innocence and experience, mundane reality and fantasy. If in previous ages the nude spoke about human consciousness through a displacement onto mythology and religion, we now find that these eternal concerns are just as easily located in our everyday worlds.

A perhaps more amorphous, but nonetheless compelling, theme than the local, is that of identity. Although removing one's clothes is an easy way to strip oneself of the fashionable signs of economic and / or regional status, the body itself is primary evidence of who we are. Laura Aguilar's hefty landscape studies, like Joe Cavallaro's engagingly goofy self-portrait, remind us that ethnic and sexual identity privilege different ideals. Both Harriet Casdin-Silver and John Coplans have recorded their own aging bodies in celebration of their longevity and in protest against social norms equating beauty with youth. John O'Reilly's collages constantly speak to his embodied desires, while Harriet Liebowitz's photographs testify to the ongoing celebration of a classicizing male nude within gay discourse. These few examples convincingly argue that for many artists and their audiences late in the century, the nude is both an eternal and timely subject that combines professional ambition with personal subjectivity.

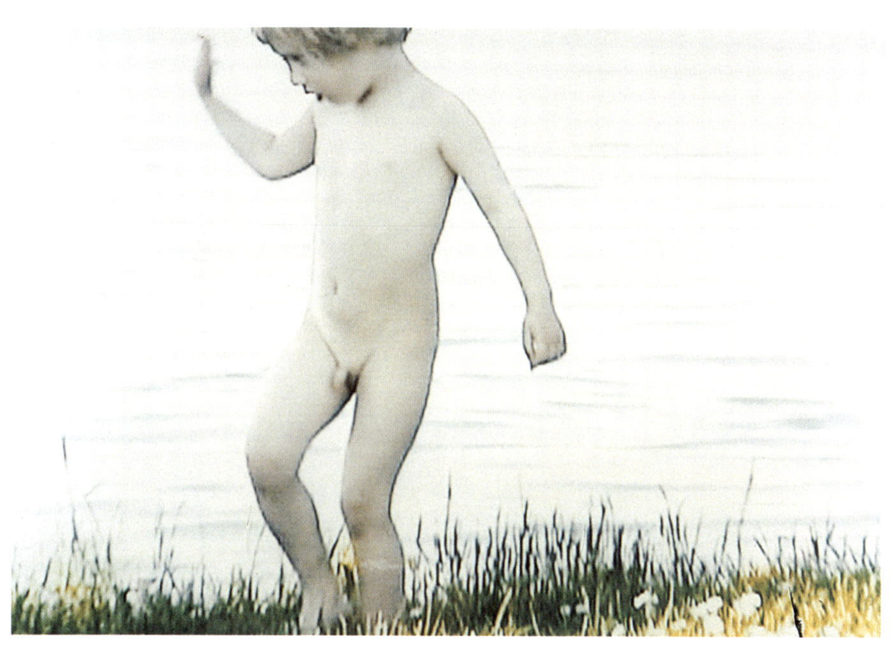

Annelies Štrba

Ån 3, 1998

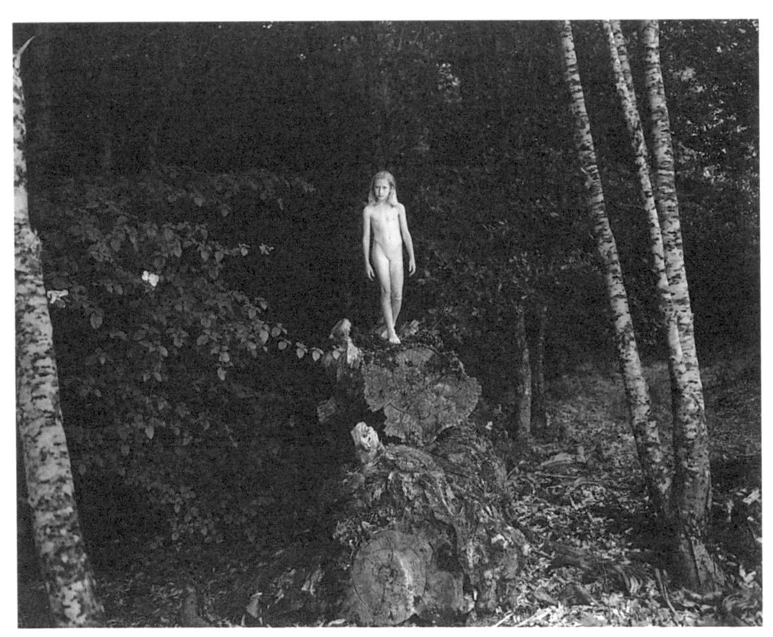

Jock Sturges

Haley; Northern California, 1995

In 1999 the nude continues to be a subject that runs from the banal to the transcendent. It thrives in paintings on black velvet, while still gracing the walls of the Uffizi and the Louvre. It remains both ancient in its pedigree and absolutely contemporary in its usefulness. The nude is a constant guide, a fixed subject that is also ideally situated to register topical concerns because it is an accepted and suitable representation of the human body. It is a projection of our fears, desires, pleasures and pains, of our lives as we know them and as we would like them to be. Still a darling of artists and sometimes a necessary element of success, the nude is our mirror and our lamp, telling us who we are in all of our variety, while also holding forth the possibility of communing with the eternal.

Notes

1. Charles Baudelaire, "The Salon of 1846," in *Art in Paris 1845—1862: Salons and Other Exhibitions*, trans. Jonathan Mayne (London: Phaidon Press, 1965), 119.

2. Baudelaire, *Art in Paris*, 117.

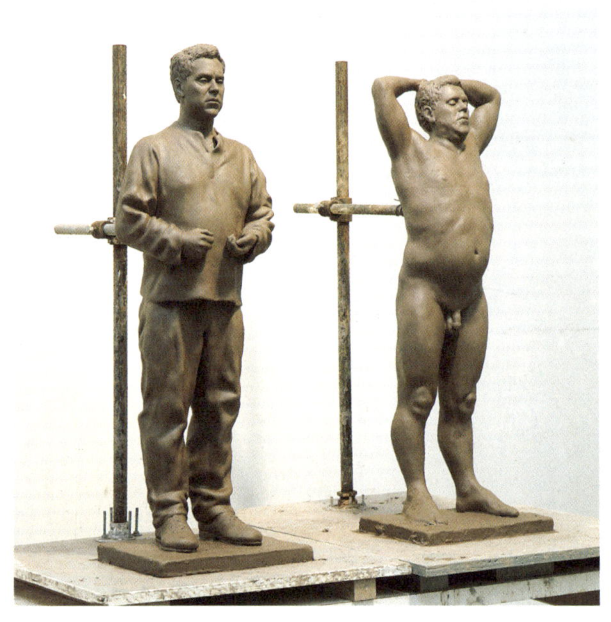

Robert Taplin

All of Me (Double Self-Portrait), (work in progress), 1999

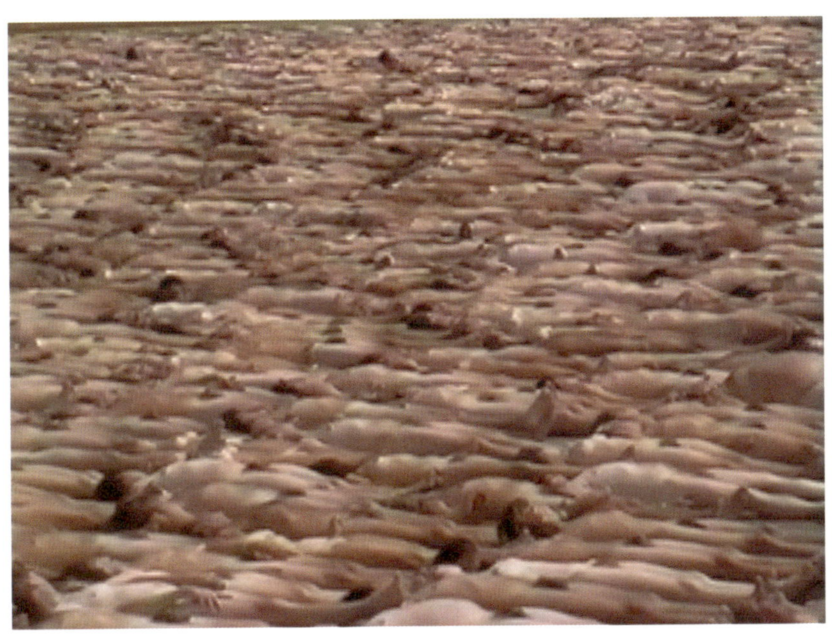

Spencer Tunick with Chris Habib

Dermafluxus (video still), from *Reaction Zone Series*, 1998

3. Baudelaire, 119.

4. Ibid.

5. Kenneth Clark, *The Nude: A Study in Ideal Form* (Princeton, New Jersey: Princeton University Press, 1956), 3.

6. Clark, *The Nude*, 3.

7. *The Metamorphoses of Ovid*, trans. Mary M. Innes (New York: Penguin Books, 1955), 231.

8. *The Elder Pliny's Chapters on the History of Art*, trans. K. Jex-Blake (Chicago: Argonaut, 1968), 109.

9. See Sarah Faunce and Linda Nochlin, *Courbet Reconsidered* (Brooklyn, New York: The Brooklyn Museum, 1988), 114.

10. On Picasso and Matisse, see Linda Nochlin and Yve-Alain Bois, "Picasso and Matisse: A Gentle Rivalry," *Artforum* 37 (February 1999), 70–77, 114–15.

11. Mark Twain, *A Tramp Abroad* (New York: The Heritage Press, 1966), 353–54.

12. Twain, *A Tramp Abroad*, 354.

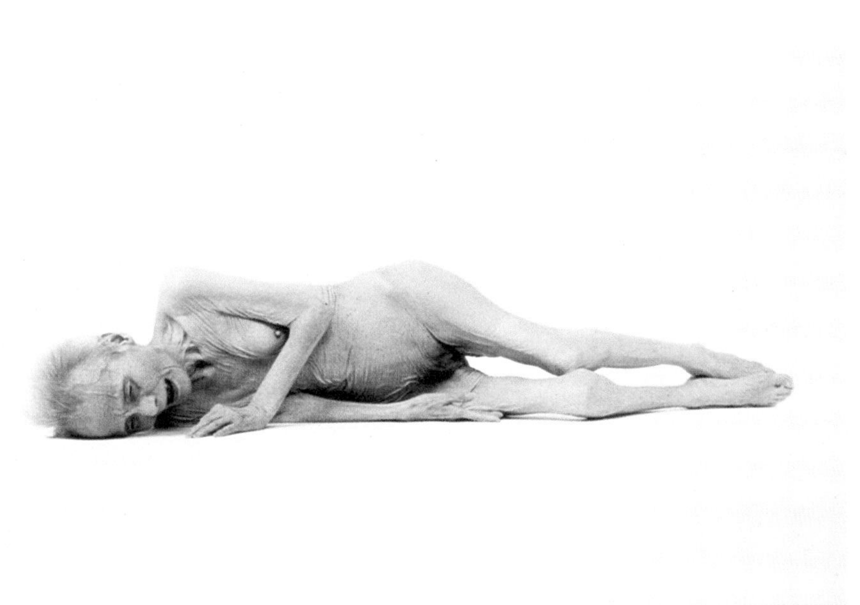

Manabu Yamanaka

Gyahtei #5, 1995

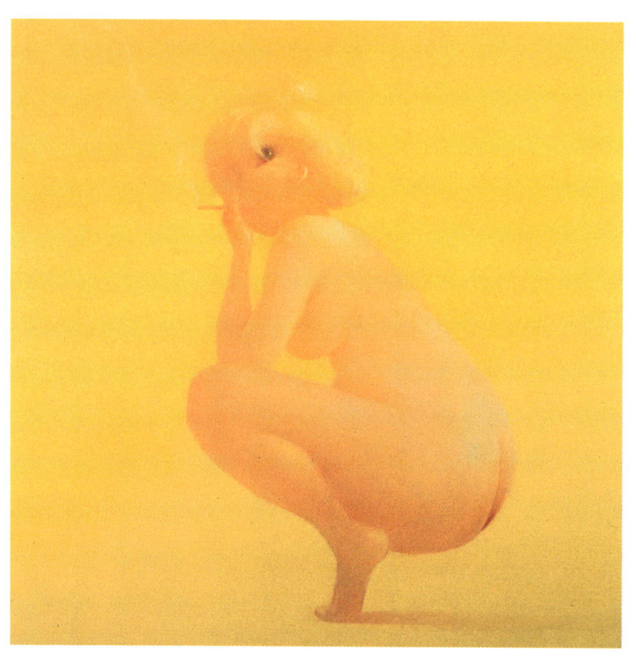

Lisa Yuskavage

Big Blonde Squatting, 1994

WORKS IN THE EXHIBITION

(All dimensions h x w x d in inches)

Laura Aguilar

Clothed/Unclothed Series No. 16, 1992
silver gelatin print, diptych, 20×32 overall

Clothed/Unclothed Series No. 34, 1994
silver gelatin print, diptych, 20 × 32 overall

Nature Self-Portrait No. 4, 1996
silver gelatin print, 16 × 20

Nature Self-Portrait No. 7, 1996
silver gelatin print, 16 × 20

Courtesy of the artist

Tina Barney

Nude #1030, 1996
chromogenic print, 16 × 20

Nude #1045, 1996
chromogenic print, 16 × 20

Nude #1058, 1996
chromogenic print, 16 × 20

Nude #1060, 1996
chromogenic print, 16 × 20

Courtesy Janet Borden, Inc., New York

Lisa Bartolozzi

Wisdom, 1998
oil on panel, 52.25 × 57.5
Courtesy Forum Gallery, New York

William Beckman

*Yellow Painting
(Man and Woman),* 1991–96
oil on panel, 90 × 80
Courtesy Forum Gallery, New York

Brett Bigbee

Bird I, 1998
graphite on paper, 48 × 30

Bird II, 1998–99
oil on canvas, 54 × 37.5
Collection of Hank Muchnic, New York

Courtesy Tibor de Nagy Gallery, New York

Paul Cadmus

Jon Extracting a Splinter NM255, 1993
crayon on Canson paper, 18.25 × 22

Male Nude Z26, 1998
crayon on gray Strathmore paper
toned with india ink and rust brown
acrylic, 14.5 × 20.63

Reclining Nude NM203, 1987
crayon on Roma Fabriano paper
20 × 17.38

Study for Shame!, 1991–92
pencil, pen, ink, and crayon on
tracing paper, 24 × 11.13

Courtesy DC Moore Gallery, New York

Sherry Camhy

Richard, The Golem, 1999
pencil on paper, 48 × 72
Courtesy of the artist

David Carbone

Visitation, 1995–96
oil on canvas, 37 × 29
Collection of Robert A. Roth

Harriet Casdin-Silver

To Soutine and Matisse, 1996
reflection holograms and C-type prints
on metal, 96 × 78
Camera person: Todd Gieg
Courtesy of the artist

Joe Cavallaro

Small Nude Man, 1994
gouache on paper, 13 × 10

Small Nude Woman, 1994
gouache on paper, 13 × 10

Courtesy Feature, Inc., New York

Eteri Chkadua

Janna, 1992
oil on canvas, 38 × 52
Courtesy Stefan Stux Gallery, New York

Chuck Close

Torso I & II, 1999
pigment prints on canvas mounted
on aluminun, 2 panels, 69 × 48 each
Courtesy PaceWildensteinMacGill, New York

John Coplans

Seated Figure, no. 4, 1987
photograph on Polaroid Positive/
Negative film, 48 × 70
Collection of T. Haddad and
M. Dembowski, Boston
Courtesy Howard Yezerski Gallery, Boston

Renée Cox

Adam, 1995
silver gelatin print, 40 × 60

Eve, 1995
silver gelatin print, 40 × 60

Courtesy of the artist

Meg Cranston

The Average American, 1996
C-print, 70.5 × 37
Published by Muse [x] Editions,
Los Angeles
Courtesy Rosamund Felsen Gallery,
Santa Monica

James Croak

Man and Woman, 1998
cast dirt, 72 × 58 × 25
Courtesy of the artist and
Stefan Stux Gallery, New York

John Currin

Three Friends, 1998
oil on linen, 78 × 61
Collection of Wendy Evans Joseph
Courtesy Andrea Rosen Gallery, New York

Steven DiGiovanni

Coin Toss, 1998
oil on canvas, 60 × 50
Courtesy of the artist

Jeanne Dunning

Puddle I, 1997
Cibachromes mounted to Plexiglas
and frames, 2 panels, 49 × 38.25 each
Collection of Joe Barron, New York

Untitled with Food, 1996
Cibachrome mounted to Plexiglas
and frame, 42.25 × 28.25

Courtesy Feigen Contemporary, New York

Karen Finley

Go Figure, 1997 and ongoing
installation
Courtesy of the artist

Lucian Freud

Girl Holding Her Foot, 1985
etching, 35 × 23.38

Naked Man on a Bed, 1990
etching, 23 × 22.5

Courtesy Marlborough Gallery, New York

Philip Grausman

Figure Study, 1988
pencil drawing, 15 × 22

Figure Study, 1996
pencil drawing, 15 × 22

Figure Study, 1996
pencil drawing, 15 × 22

Reclining Figure, 1983
pewter, 6 × 11.25 × 23.5

Courtesy of the artist

Anne Harris

Third Portrait with Max, 1996–97
oil on canvas, 46 × 30
Private Collection
Courtesy DC Moore Gallery, New York

Twin Study, 1998
pastel, charcoal and graphite
on toned paper, 24.63 × 22.5
Collection of Bowdoin College
Museum of Art, Brunswick, ME

Jacqueline Hayden

Ancient Statuary Series #2, 1997
platinum palladium print, 5 × 4

Ancient Statuary Series #4, 1997
platinum palladium print, 5.5 × 3.75

Ancient Statuary Series #10, 1998
platinum palladium print, 6.5 × 4.4

Courtesy Howard Yezerski Gallery, Boston

Kinke Kooi

Fool, 1990
acrylic, pencil on paper, 16.5 × 11.6
Collection of P.G. Van Deursen

Hairy Woman, 1992
pencil on paper, 25.59 × 19.69
Collection of The Museum of
Modern Art, Arnhem, The Netherlands

Menstruating Woman, 1992
acrylic, pencil on paper , 16.54 × 11.61
Collection of Ms. Kooi-De Wal

Courtesy Feature, Inc., New York

Peter Krashes

Untitled Series #1, 1996
oil on linen, 59 × 39

Untitled Series #3, 1996
oil on linen, 59 × 39

Courtesy of the artist

Daniel Ladd

Silenus, (reduction and fragment), 1998
Attributed to Lysippos, 3rd Century B.C.,
Vatican Museum
Two dried hard-shell gourds
grown in molds, 23 inches

Venus of Willendorf, 1998
Prehistoric European fertility goddess,
enlarged to scale

Dried hard-shell gourd grown
in a mold, 13 inches

Courtesy of the artist

Jacob Lawrence

Figure Study After Vesalius, 1974
pencil on paper, 8 × 6

*Standing Man with
Hammer and Plane*, 1996
pencil on paper, 9.5 × 6.5

Standing Man with Plumb-Bob, 1996
pencil on paper, 9.5 × 6.5

Standing Man with Right Angle, 1996
pencil on paper, 9.5 × 6.5

Courtesy DC Moore Gallery, New York

Harriet Leibowitz

Larry I, 1995
silver gelatin print, 20 × 24

Larry II, 1995
silver gelatin print, 20 × 24

Courtesy of the artist

Michael Leonard

Female Bather on Gold II, 1989
alkyd oil on masonite, 26 × 27.5

Male Bather, 1989
alkyd oil on masonite, 25 × 27.5

Courtesy Forum Gallery, New York

Melanie Manchot

With Mountains I, 1999
C-print, 58.66 × 61.42
Courtesy Galerie/
edition Lutz Fiebig, Berlin

With Mountains I (detail), 1999
Digital spray jet on nylon-reinforced
vinyl fabric, 11 × 21 feet
Courtesy of the artist

Denise Marika

Battle, 1994–1995
C-prints and steel ship channels,
seven units, 84 × 4.5 × 3 each
Collection of Rose Art Museum,
Brandeis University, Waltham, MA;
Hays Acquisition Fund, 1995
Courtesy Howard Yezerski Gallery, Boston

John O'Reilly

As An Apollo, 1981
Photo and halftone montage
9.81 × 6.13
Courtesy Howard Yezerski Gallery, Boston

Between Three Mirrors, 1986
Polaroid collage
3.69 × 6.88
Courtesy Stephen Daiter Gallery, Chicago

Dutch Bedroom, 1997
Polaroid collage, 6.5 × 6.25
Courtesy Howard Yezerski Gallery, Boston

Posing for Bonnard, 1985
Polaroid montage
3.44 × 4.75
Courtesy Todd Hosfelt Gallery, San Francisco

Talking with Whitman, 1984
Polaroid collage, 6.5 × 3.69
Courtesy Julie Saul Gallery, New York

With Two Shepherds, 1985
Polaroid collage, 3.19 × 5.81
Courtesy Fletcher/Priest Gallery,
Worcester, MA

Hanneline Røgeberg

Ex-It, 1995
oil on canvas, 96 × 48
Courtesy of the artist

Karin Sander

Clemens 1:5, 1999
3-dimensional scan of the original person
FDM (Fused Deposition Modelling),
ABS plastic
13.38 high
Courtesy of the Artist

Jenny Saville

Untitled, 1994
oil on canvas, 112 × 66
Collection of Susan Kasen Summer
and Robert D. Summer

Andres Serrano

Budapest (The Lake), 1994
Cibachrome, silicone, Plexiglas,
wood frame, 65.25 × 54.75 × .75
Courtesy Paula Cooper Gallery, New York

Robert Stivers

Series 5 (two figures), 1994
silver gelatin print, 16 × 20

Self-Portrait, 1991–94
silver gelatin print, 16 × 20

Courtesy Yancey Richardson Gallery, New York

Annelies Štrba

Ån 3, 1998
color photograph mounted
on aluminum, edition 1/3, 49.5 × 72
Collection of Martin Margulies,
Key Biscayne, FL
Courtesy Bill Maynes Gallery, New York

Jock Sturges

2 Alexandras, Jeanne, Marine et Gäelle;
Montalivet, France, 1987
silver gelatin print, 16 × 20

Haley; Northern California, 1995
silver gelatin print, 16 × 20

Courtesy Yancey Richardson Gallery, New York

Robert Taplin

All of Me (Double Self-Portrait), 1999
Concrete on wood base, 65 × 48 × 24
Courtesy of the artist

Spencer Tunick with Chris Habib

Dermafluxus, 1998
from *Reaction Zone Series*
projected video, approx. 8 minutes
Courtesy 1–20 Gallery, New York

Manabu Yamanaka

Gyahtei #1, 1995
68 × 31.5
black and white photograph

Gyahtei #5, 1995
68 × 31.5
black and white photograph

Courtesy Stefan Stux Gallery, New York

Lisa Yuskavage

Big Blonde Squatting, 1994
oil on linen, 112 × 66
Collection of Yvonne Force Inc.,
Courtesy Marianne Boesky Gallery, New York

Photo Credits:

Page 26: Todd Gieg

Pages 30, 56, 57 and 58: Karen Finley installation
presented as part of *Uncommon Sense,*
March 16–July 6, 1997, courtesy MoCA at
The Geffen Contemporary, Los Angeles.
Pages 30, 56 and 57: photos by Paula Goldman;
page 58: photo by Lyle Ashton Harris.

Pages 34 and 35: Oren Slor

Page 51: Fred Scruton

Page 61: Ivan Dalla Tana

Page 65: Greg Heins

THE ALDRICH MUSEUM OF CONTEMPORARY ART

Founded 1964

Chairman's Circle

Mr. and Mrs. Larry Aldrich
Alexander Julian Foundation
    for Aesthetic Understanding
    & Appreciation
Emily and Richard Buckingham
Connecticut Commission on
    the Arts
Teresa and Jeffrey Furman–
    Fortrend International, LLC
Anna-Maria and Stephen M. Kellen
Mr. Henry Leir

Lini and Louis J. Lipton
Sherry Hope and Joel Mallin
Mr. Douglas F. Maxwell
O'Grady Family Foundation
Sheila and Charles Perrin,
    Perrin Family Foundation
RJR Nabisco, Inc.
Martin and Toni Sosnoff Foundation
Sotheby's
Drs. Marc J. and Livia Straus
Genevieve and Richard Tucker
Judy and Peter Wasserman

Benefactor

Walter H. Annenberg, Harriett Ames
    Charitable Trust
Dede and James Bartlett
étant dónnes, The French
    American Endowment for
    Contemporary Art
Carol and Arthur Goldberg
Sunny and Brad Goldberg
Sandy and Leonard Gubar
Shelby White and Leon Levy
Mr. Perry J. Lewis and Basha Szymanska

Ms. Vera List
Pepsi-Cola Co.
Mr. and Mrs. F. F. Randolph, Jr.
The Reader's Digest Association, Inc.
Mr. and Mrs. Warren Rubin–
    Workbench, Inc.
    of Greenwich, Westport,
    Scarsdale & Danbury
Dr. and Mrs. Harvey Sadow

Patron

Ann and Steven Ames
Caroline and Richard Anderson
Atalanta/Sosnoff Capital Corp.
Frank E. Baxter
Boehringer Ingelheim Corp.
Marianne Boesky Fine Art
Alice Saligman and Klaus Brinkman
Dr. Brian Clark–
    Schlumberger-Doll Research
Mr. Stephen B. Brown
David R. Collens–Storm King
    Art Center
Patton R. Corrigan–The Stamford
    Capital Group, Inc.

Jeanne and Richard Fisher
Joyce Lowinson Kootz and
    Helmut N. Friedlaender
Mindy and Laurence Friedman
Pamela and Robert Goergen–
    The Ropart Group
Marianne Goodman Gallery
The Gordon F Linke and Jocelyn B
    Linke Foundation
Mr. and Mrs. Gregory Holt,–
    Daybrook Resources, Corp.
Housatonic Valley Travel Commission
Jill and Ken Iscol
Katonah Art Museum
Mary and Robert Kidder
Sandy and Harlan P. Kleiman
Carolyn Labutka–AON Foundation
Jo Carole and Ronald S. Lauder
Mr. Peter Malkin
Marlborough Gallery
Carol and Raymond Merritt
Robert Miller Gallery
Deanne and Richard Mincer
Mr. and Mrs. Jerry Minsky

Mr. and Mrs. Lester Morse, Jr.–
    Morse Family Foundation
Nash Family Foundation, Inc.
Ann and Martin Rabinowitz
Ridgefield Bank
The Richard and Hinda,
    Rosenthal Foundation
Saks Fifth Avenue
Samuel Zell Foundation
Hannelore and R.B. Schulhof
Agnes Gund and Daniel Shapiro
Renate and Sidney Shapiro
Dr. and Mrs. Robert Soley
Mr. Arthur Stern III
Mr. and Mrs. Anthony Ullmann
Jean and David Wallace
Mr. Leonard Wien
Mr. and Mrs. Mark Wheless

Director's Circle

Mr. and Mrs. Ralph Ablon
Mr. and Mrs. Stefan Abrams
Jill Weinberg Adams and
    Thomas Adams–Lennon,
    Weinberg, Inc.

Glenn Bailey
Madeleine and Jay Bennett
Bonakdar Jancou Gallery
Mr. Henry Buhl, III
Chancellor Park at Laurelwood
Eileen and Michael Cohen
Paula Cooper Gallery
Zoe and Joel Dictrow
Phyllis and Donald Duberstein
Mr. Martin Edelston–
    Boardroom, Inc.
Jody and Stuart Eichner
Andre Emmerich Gallery
Gail and Al Engelberg
Ursula and Peter Evans
Nancy and A. Robert Faesy
Ronald Feldman Gallery
Joni Weyl and Sidney Felsen–
    Gemini G.E.L.
Cheryl and Robert Fishko–
    Forum Gallery
Mr. and Mrs. Joel Freedman
Eve and Theodore Friedman
Galerie LeLong

Barbara Gladstone Gallery
Robert Gober
Mr. and Mrs. Stuart Green
Ursula Von Rydinsvard and
    Paul Greengard
Mr. Leo Guthman
Mr. Andrew Hall
Barbara and Rod R. Hamachek
Barbara Handman, People for
    the American Way
Mr. Peter Hoffman–Duracell
    International Inc.
Mr. Rolf Heitmeyer
Mr. and Mrs. Paul L. Herring
Mr. and Mrs. Harry Huberth
Ms. Nash Hyon
Mr. Robert Kidder
Hedy and Kent Klineman
Werner Kramarsky
Luhring Augustine Gallery
Susan and David Marco
Bill Maynes Gallery
Marlborough Gallery

Robert Miller Gallery
Mr. Roger Mudre–
    The Ridgefield Guild
    of Artists
New York Community Trust
Mr. and Mrs. Walter Northup
PaceWildenstein
People's Bank
Ellen and Robert Perless
Yvonne and Leslie Pollack
Marianne and Ed Pollak
Nancy and Joel Portney
Andrea and Andrew Potash
Mr. and Mrs. Alan Safir
St. Onge, Steward,
    Johnston & Reens
Mr. Stanley B. Scheinman
Stephen Haller Gallery, Inc.
Barbara Schwartz
Stephanie and Abram Shnay
Sheila and Ramsey Siegel
Sue and Marco Stoffel
Mr. Laurie Tisch Sussman
Mark Theran